———————————*———————————

*The
Iron Will
of
Jefferson
Davis*

Jefferson Davis during his term as U.S. Senator

CASS CANFIELD

---★---

THE IRON WILL OF JEFFERSON DAVIS

---★---

HARCOURT BRACE JOVANOVICH

NEW YORK AND LONDON

—————————————— ✳ ——————————————

*Endpapers, "The Burning of Richmond," are reproduced by
permission of the Valentine Museum, Richmond, Virginia.*

Printed in the United States of America

Library of Congress Cataloging in Publication Data

*Canfield, Cass, 1897–
The iron will of Jefferson Davis.*

*Bibliography: p.
1. Davis, Jefferson, 1808–1889. 2. Statesmen—
United States—Biography. 3. Confederate States of
America—Presidents—Biography. I. Title.
E467.1.D26C3   973.7'13'0924 [B]   78–53908*
ISBN *0–15–145642–9*

First edition

B C D E

---✶---

TO THOMAS CASS CANFIELD

---*---

Preface

No man in American history had to face heavier odds and greater discouragements than Jefferson Davis. No man, I believe, could have held together the Confederacy as long as he did; under crushing defeats his indomitable will held firm.

As President of the Confederacy and commander-in-chief of its armies, he directed the war effort of the South. Accordingly, I have devoted considerable space to the furious campaigns of the Civil War.

The comment of the *London Times* toward the end of hostilities gives a vivid picture of the magnitude of this conflict. "The Americans are making war as no people ever made it before. Their campaigns combine the costliness of modern expeditions with the carnage of barbaric invasions. Grant squanders life like Attila, and money like Louis XIV."

For enormously helpful research and for some passages included in this book—notably on the institution of slavery and on the shortages of much needed supplies in the Confederacy —I am indebted to Joan H. King; for editorial advice I owe thanks to Bruce Catton and to Mariana Fitzpatrick.

Of the biographies of Jefferson Davis which I have consulted, the most useful were *Jefferson Davis* by Robert McElroy, a three-volume biography of Davis by Hudson Strode, and Allen Tate's *Jefferson Davis: His Rise and Fall.*

Contents

Illustrations

Illustrations

———————————————★—————————————

The
Iron Will
of
Jefferson
Davis

1

---*---

Youth and Young Manhood 1808-1835

In 1851, who would not have welcomed the opportunity to come and see what a prosperous and promising country this was? There were, of course, a few clouds on the horizon. The question of where the new transcontinental railroad would pass had already provoked among Jefferson Davis and others heated discussions on the Senate floor, as had the proposed Kansas-Nebraska bill. But neither issue would come up for vote for several years. In Brunswick, Maine, the relatively unknown Harriet Beecher Stowe was writing the final chapters of her explosive book, *Uncle Tom's Cabin*—a fictional story of slavery which was serialized in *The National Era* in June of that same year. But by and large, the future looked rosy. Henry Clay had just announced that the Fugitive Slave Act was being enforced (everywhere except in Boston); America was no longer at war and had recently acquired California and the Southwest territories. Furthermore, gold had been discovered in the Far West, and by 1851 some $55 million per annum was being extracted from the mines. On the surface, at least, America was a unified country. It seemed a time to rejoice.

Few Americans—apart from isolated fanatics on both sides —wanted a civil war, even fewer considered the possibility of one. Southerners were convinced of the merits of their way of life. After all, it was to the advantage of any master to take an interest in the welfare of his slaves; they were part of his capital. Hospital-trained doctors and nurses were sometimes employed on large plantations to care for the cotton hands.

In January, 1851, two men who were to dominate American politics ten years later were in temporary eclipse. Jefferson Davis had just suffered the only political defeat of his career—the contest for the governorship of Mississippi; and Abraham Lincoln, having lost his bid for the Commissioner of the General Land Office, was preparing to erase what then seemed to remain of his political career. The two leaders and antagonists in the Civil War came from very different backgrounds, and each reflected his own. Yet on the question of slavery, which so agitated the country in the 1840's and 1850's, they shared many views. Both feared the effects of hasty emancipation. In fact, during the debates with Stephen A. Douglas, Lincoln declared he was willing to wait a hundred years for the complete destruction of slavery, if only he could be certain that it was "in the process of ultimate extinction." In addition, both believed that the institution of slavery, so long as it existed, should enjoy the same protection as property. Where they differed was how the extension of slavery into new territory in the West would affect the country. Davis held that this would hasten the solution of the problem by diffusing the slave population, while Lincoln took the opposite position.

Both these future leaders were born in Kentucky—Jefferson Davis in 1808, eight months before Lincoln. The youngest of ten children, Davis was descended from John Davis, who had migrated to America from Wales. Jefferson's father, Samuel Davis, fought as a captain in Georgia during the Revolution, receiving 1,200 acres of land at the war's end for his services.

Subsequently elected Clerk of the Courts, from which he derived a decent income, he married a handsome Scotch-Irish girl, Jane Cook. According to family legend, she was the niece of the famous Revolutionary general, Nathanael Greene.

Jefferson Davis's mother was known for her beauty and brains. Jefferson described his father as "unusually handsome . . . an accomplished horseman . . . usually grave and stoical . . . and of such sound judgement that his opinions were law to his children. . . ."

After spending a few years on his Georgia farm, Samuel Davis chose to live in Kentucky, where he obtained 600 acres and settled down to breed blood horses. Four years later the family moved to Mississippi, where Jefferson's early memories were of Poplar Grove, a simple house near the town of Woodville. This was a country of gamblers and lawbreakers. Bear and wild hogs roamed the swamps.

When Jefferson was five, Samuel sent him to a nearby log cabin school, where the boy did poorly. After two years it was decided to send him North to a school run by the Dominican Fathers; the long journey through Indian country to Washington County, Kentucky, was an adventure. The three years he spent at the Saint Thomas Aquinas school made him very sympathetic toward Roman Catholicism, so much so that he came close to adopting the faith—which is surprising, since he had been brought up a Baptist. He actually told Father Wilson, the school's head, that he wished to become a Catholic; Wilson smiled and suggested that for the time being he had better eat some Catholic food. Thereafter Jefferson joined no church until he was past fifty, when he was confirmed an Episcopalian.

Now ten, Jefferson returned to Mississippi, where he attended Wilkinson Academy. He proved ill disposed toward learning and resentful of the stern discipline imposed by the principal. When he consulted his father, Samuel said, "It is for

THE FAMOUS JARRETT & PALMER LONDON COMP

CONSOLI

W.J. MORGAN & CO. LITH. CLEVELAND.O.

UNCLE TO

Poster for production

SLAVINS ORIGINAL AMERICAN TROUPE

D WITH

1'S CABIN.

of Uncle Tom's Cabin

you to elect whether you will work with head or hands. My son could not be an idler." Jefferson chose "hands" and was assigned a cotton-picking job. But after a day in the burning Mississippi sun he shifted to "head" and was allowed to return to school, where his work improved, showing that he had learned his lesson.

Jefferson, at the age of fifteen, was sent for a classical education to Transylvania College at Lexington, Kentucky, one of the best schools in the East. He studied Greek and Latin diligently, despite occasional mischief-making. He was quick, alert, sensitive, and fiercely loyal to his friends.

Three years later his father died. Upon hearing the news, Jefferson wrote to his sister: "Dear Sister: It is gratifying to hear from a friend—but the intelligence contained in yours was more than sufficient to mar the satisfaction of hearing from anyone. You must imagine, I cannot describe, the shock my feelings sustained at the sad intelligence."

Having written this stiff letter, Jefferson entered West Point in 1824. Yet he had no inclination for a military life, and wished to become a lawyer. Among his fellow students were Robert E. Lee ("who was noted at the Academy for his humorless rectitude"), Davis's good friend Albert Sidney Johnston, and Joseph E. Johnston, all three of whom became generals in the Confederate army. Another boon companion of Jefferson's, Robert Anderson, would be the major in command of Fort Sumter at the start of the Civil War. Jefferson was "distinguished in the corps for his manly bearing," according to Allen Tate in his biography *Jefferson Davis: His Rise and Fall*. He had a fine, if rather robust, figure, offset by a gay, easygoing manner. He drank sufficiently to be court-martialed along with some of his friends.

The routine at West Point was severe: nine hours a day were

devoted to recitations, and two to four hours to drill and military exercises. One day in class a practice fireball was accidentally ignited, causing the instructor to shout, "All hands, run for your lives!" Jefferson contemptuously picked up the hissing bomb and flung it out the window. His teachers admired the boy's courage but found him hard to handle; he was pugnacious and high-spirited, and received many demerits.

On another occasion Jefferson escaped serious trouble when he and his fellow cadets planned an illegal Christmas party, at which they proposed to demonstrate how to make spiked eggnog. Among the guests were Lee and Joseph Johnston. When the great moment of tasting arrived, the authorities showed up and sent Cadet Davis to his quarters under arrest. Luckily, he missed the riot that followed; it developed into a free fight between students and officials. One officer was chased to his quarters with a drawn sword, and Jefferson's roommate, Walter Guion, got hold of a pistol and tried to shoot a captain. Nineteen cadets were court-martialed and dismissed.

Jefferson and Joseph Johnston were both smitten with the local tavern keeper's pretty daughter, so they went to old Fort Putnam to settle their dispute by fisticuffs. Johnston, the heavier of the two, won the battle, and the two men were at odds from that day on.

When he graduated from the Academy, Jefferson Davis stood twenty-third out of thirty-three. This undistinguished showing was partly due to his passion for extracurricular reading on every conceivable subject. His checkered West Point career made his future look uncertain, but his years there had imbued him with a high sense of honor and duty. And West Point had taught him something else: only trained soldiers win in war.

———————————

Mississippi lay in the center of the Cotton Kingdom, which included South Carolina, Georgia, Alabama, Mississippi, Florida, and Louisiana. Eli Whitney's invention of the cotton gin in 1793 laid the basis of the fortunes in that area. Had it not been for their prosperity and resulting strength, these states would have had no choice but to remain loyal to the Union, since they would have lacked the power to resist the North.

The early planters of the era of Washington and Thomas Jefferson had developed an elitist outlook, feeding on the novels of Walter Scott. The Old South was an aristocratic, landowning society, an area different from any other. In the words of H. J. Eckenrode, in his *Jefferson Davis President of the South*, it was "African jungle in part; medieval Europe in part; American democracy in part . . . the strangest imaginable compound of ages and ideas and for that reason fascinating."

In Virginia people generally remained in the class to which they had been born, but in the Lower South men were on the make, so that a society of *nouveaux riches*—the owners of big plantations—developed. They wintered in New Orleans, where the social season was the most brilliant in the country; the first American city to have opera, it was in close cultural contact with Paris.

In this society of the Lower South only a minority was really wealthy. Most of the people were small farmers living in two-room log houses. An early nineteenth-century American census described the average Southerner as a farmer who owned a small amount of land which he cultivated with the assistance of his wife and children; they were the "poor whites." Above them were the tenant farmers, artisans, and professional men, as well as a number of large plantation owners. Some Southerners were convinced that their social status depended on the number of slaves they owned, but they were in the minority. By 1860, 385,000 families owned slaves, while over a million and a half did not; fewer than 3,000 families owned more than one hundred slaves.

Since approximately three-quarters of the Southern whites kept no slaves, the question arises as to why they chose to fight for slavery. The answer seems to be that by establishing the inferiority of the black man, the non-slave owner hoped to become a member of a superior caste. Also, many Southern non-slave owners feared a Negro insurrection and therefore backed the Confederate cause, and some supported slavery because it was part of the Establishment. (Other whites—some of whom owned plantations—felt it ridiculous to spend their time in useless attacks upon institutions that would die themselves.)

Hierarchy was strictly observed in plantation households: house servants, pastry cooks, laundresses and seamstresses, stable and garden hands, and chief dairywomen, in that order; often as many as two hundred "agriculturalists" followed in tribal rank. The health and general well-being of a slave varied according to whether he or she was owned by a benevolent or cruel master. Blacks assigned to the cotton fields worked fifteen to sixteen hours a day with only a few minutes' break for a meal of little more than corn.

Slave trading had almost died out by the mid-nineteenth century, though a few planters continued to purchase slaves. In the late 1850's a fourteen-year-old girl was bought in Tennessee for $1,000; male slaves were sold for half as much again as females. Slaves were priced according to the current cotton market. For example, if cotton was quoted at 12¢ on the market, the Negro male was worth $1,200; but if prices jumped 3¢, his value became $1,500. In general, the Southern slave plantation was efficient and more productive than Northern agriculture.

11

The Davis family prospered, largely due to the ability of Joseph, Jefferson's older brother by twenty-three years. When his father died, Joseph had become head of the family and a father to Jefferson. He was a distinguished lawyer as well as a big plantation owner.

Upon leaving West Point, Jefferson Davis visited Joseph's home in Warren County, Mississippi. From there he proceeded northward with Joseph Pemberton, his slave and lifelong devoted servant, to his first post at Jefferson Barracks in St. Louis. He arrived in 1828 and was almost immediately transferred to Fort Crawford, in Indian country to the north. Davis described his arrival: "Being . . . something of a martinet, I arrayed myself in full uniform and made my way to the regimental headquarters."

Jefferson's army duty was to protect settlers from the Indians —dangerous work. The winters were severe; during a particularly bad one he almost died of pneumonia. Pemberton nursed him back to health, but Davis never recovered his full strength and thereafter frequently caught colds that developed into severe neuralgia and even blinded him for several days.

Colonel Zachary Taylor was in command at Fort Crawford, and Jefferson Davis started to court his beautiful and spirited eighteen-year-old daughter, Sarah Knox Taylor. Unfortunately, the colonel did not favor his suit, partly because the reckless young lieutenant, according to a memoir left by a Pottawattomi chief, had been invited to a tribal wedding and made advances there to a young squaw of great personal attraction who danced gracefully in her Indian style. Fascinated with her charms, Lieutenant Davis danced with her in almost every set and even asked the musicians to change a quadrille to a waltz so he could put his arms around her waist. Then, freeing himself from her, he jerked and swayed to and fro, yelling at the top of his voice, in imitation of the Indians present. Colonel Taylor,

Joseph Emory Davis, brother of Jefferson Davis

who took no part in the dance, sat looking on, almost splitting his sides with laughter. But the young squaw, misinterpreting this, grew indignant, and her brother, a tall, athletic Indian, became very angry and determined to punish the offender. In a drunken rage the young buck went up to Lieutenant Davis, tweaked his nose, and accused him of insulting his sister. Davis pushed the Indian, drawing his pistol at the same time that the Indian drew a long scalping knife from its scabbard. The dance stopped, the women screamed, and all was confusion and alarm; everyone expected to see the death of one or both, but Colonel Taylor sprang between the combatants, preventing bloodshed. After this, Zachary Taylor became even more doubtful about the young officer who was so determined to win his daughter's hand.

Taylor's view in this matter was hardened by a difference of opinion in a court-martial, in which Davis voted against the colonel's wishes on a matter of military punctilio. The court-martial consisted of Colonel Taylor, Major Thomas Smith, Lieutenant Davis, and a lieutenant who had recently arrived. The new officer asked to be excused from wearing his full-dress uniform at the trial; Taylor, a stickler for army etiquette, voted against the lieutenant's request, but Smith and Davis voted yes. This annoyed Colonel Taylor, who then forbade Jefferson to enter his house, and swore he would never allow him to marry his daughter.

Almost half a century later Davis was still arguing his position: "I was right as to principle . . . but impolitic in the manner of asserting it . . . the colonel assailed me harshly. . . . Then I became wrong, as angry men are apt to be."

The Southern Code, which dictated a gentleman's behavior, was not yet dead; accordingly, Davis determined to challenge his colonel and requested his friend Captain McRee to serve as his second; but the captain told Davis that it was absurd to

Sarah Knox Taylor, first wife of Jefferson Davis

duel with the man he wanted as his father-in-law. Called into council, Mrs. McRee backed up her husband and announced that if Davis could master his temper, she would arrange from time to time for him and Miss Taylor to meet.

During the next seven years Davis served in various army posts in the old Northwest and the South. His first real military experience was in the Black Hawk War of 1832, in which whites massacred Indians, including women and children. A redeeming feature of this disgraceful war was the generous behavior of Lieutenant Jefferson Davis toward the Indian chief Black Hawk.

Lieutenant Davis took part in the pursuit of the Indian invaders, pressing them so closely that they had difficulty in gathering supplies; what the enemy did not know was that the regulars themselves were short of food. Chasing the enemy, Davis admired the gallantry and resourcefulness of Black Hawk and his followers, although Davis realized that, if captured by the Indians, he would be put to torture and then scalped.

"We were one day pursuing the Indians," he said later, "when we came close to the Wisconsin river. Reaching the river bank, the Indians made so determined a stand, and fought with such desperation, that they held us in check. During this time the squaws tore bark from the trees and made little shallops, in which they floated their papooses . . . across to an island, also swimming over the ponies. As soon as this was accomplished half of the warriors plunged in and swam across, each holding his gun in one hand over his head, and swimming with the other. As soon as they reached the opposite bank, they opened fire on us, under the cover of which the other half slipped down the bank and swam in like manner. This was the most brilliant exhibition of military tactics that I ever witnessed, a feat of most consummate management and bravery, in the face of an enemy of greatly superior numbers. . . . Had it been performed by white men it would have been immortalized as one of the most splendid achievements in military history."

With the Black Hawk War there began the removal of Indians to the trans-Mississippi area. When the war ended, Lieutenant Davis was placed in command of troops guarding Black Hawk and a hundred of his warriors, who were taken as prisoners from Fort Crawford to Rock Island and thence to Jefferson Barracks at St. Louis. Black Hawk was grateful to Davis for his protection when a crowd threatened his safety.

Soon after, Davis was promoted to first lieutenant and appointed regimental adjutant—a singular honor. He was sent away to distant Fort Gibson, on the border of Arkansas.

Two years had passed since Davis had left Fort Crawford, but he had written several letters to Knox Taylor and may have seen her more than once. Accordingly, he informed the colonel that he planned to marry his daughter as soon as it could be arranged; furthermore, Knox told her father that, since she had waited two years for his consent, she would marry without it. Colonel Taylor fumed at these announcements and exclaimed: "I will be damned if another daughter of mine shall marry into the Army. I know enough of the family life of officers; I scarcely know my own children, or they me." He then added, "I have no personal objections to Lieutenant Davis," but remained obdurate.

Finally Mrs. Gibson Taylor, Knox's aunt, pleaded Jefferson's case with her brother, who at last reluctantly agreed. The wedding took place on June 17, 1835, and two weeks later Jefferson Davis resigned his commission. He had become disillusioned with the army, and his imagination was stirred by a new invention—a contrivance that ran on tracks with an engine propelled by steam. Jefferson felt that this invention would revolutionize commerce, so he decided to go into railroading, but then abandoned the idea when his brother Joseph discouraged him. Nevertheless, Jefferson held on to his vision of a new, highly industrialized America.

Planter, Politician, Soldier
1835-1847

In July, 1835, the newlyweds journeyed to Warren County, Mississippi. They looked forward to a delightful life there, and with good reason, for the circumstances of an established Southern planter before 1860 were enviable.

Joseph had transferred to his younger brother a generous section of his own plantation, "Hurricane." Thus Jefferson, having built himself a house, became a planter, calling his place "Brierfield"—an appropriate name, since when the new owner first viewed his place, the land was covered with tangled undergrowth. The property lay in a bend of the Mississippi twenty miles below Vicksburg, and was not as healthy as Jefferson had reported. Knox's mother, who knew this area, warned her daughter not to remain at Brierfield during the fever-ridden hot season, but Knox replied, "Do not make yourself uneasy about me; the country is quite healthy." Jefferson was less sanguine; when summer came, he set out with his bride for his sister's home in Louisiana. But the malarial fever had attacked them already, and soon after their arrival both were close to death.

One night Davis was roused by singing; it was Knox, singing a song associated with the time of their courtship. She was in her last delirium and Jefferson, disregarding the doctor's orders, rose from his bed and rushed into her room. It was too late: she had passed into unconsciousness, from which she never returned. On September 15, 1835, less than three months after her marriage, she died. Jefferson suffered acutely, and in learning to bear his grief developed a stoical strain. However, though Davis had the standoffish quality of a man raised in the Southern aristocratic tradition, he made many warm friendships.

In the years that followed, Jefferson Davis led a lonely life. He joined Joseph at Hurricane and spent eight years supervising his own plantation as an absentee landlord. Gradually he recovered from the tragedy of Knox's death, and prospered. His success as a plantation manager was partly due to the way he handled his slaves. Jefferson believed that force should be used sparingly, that self-government should be encouraged; consequently, no slave was punished except after conviction by a jury of blacks. The master kept the right to modify a sentence, or to grant a pardon, and sometimes he would intervene to prevent too severe a punishment for a minor offense.

If all plantation owners had treated their slaves as Jefferson Davis did, slavery might have been considered a beneficent institution. But Davis's manner of handling his slaves did not affect his views: he maintained that God had created the Negro unequal to the white man, and that no amount of education could change this. After the Civil War Davis said: "The whites are better off for the abolition of slavery, though it is an equally patent fact that the colored people are not."

Jefferson knew by name all the black children on his plantation, who adored him and lined up morning and evening to wave and call to "Marse Jeff." His brother Joseph noticed that he could not bear to have anyone dislike him, so that if one of the blacks became annoyed with him he was not satisfied until he got back into the slave's good graces.

Slavery had become a way of life by the time of the Civil War, but the Southern plantation system had existed before slavery and did not disappear after the slaves were emancipated. The Southerners clung to their myths: a black man could raise a sugar or cotton crop better than a white; white laborers were not adapted to work under a hot sun; Africans were not able to assimilate knowledge.

Southerners believed that planters, who were usually of English ancestry, represented the superior American. They claimed that Southerners had instilled into the Constitution the liberal political ideas of the previous century, and that as a result the planter-general, George Washington, had become President. Democracy had ceased to be a drawing-room philosophy and had become a working political system for which the average man was accountable.

Northerners considered themselves cultivated and regarded their Southern neighbors as "hot-blooded, genial sportsmen who would lend their last dollar to a friend and kill him for an ill-judged word." Yet Virginians could claim that their jails were infrequently full. Whether or not slavery was responsible for this, the rarity of extreme poverty had resulted in a lower crime rate, at least in that state.

The wealthy planter was less well off than he was thought to be; few Northerners understood that much of the return of a cotton crop went into the pockets of Northern merchants who provided the necessary manufactured equipment without which the crops could not be successfully produced. But many Southerners knew this, and resented the fact that much of their labor served to enrich the North.

The plantation managers were among the first to be affected by the Civil War. Following the Confederate conscription bill of 1862, many of these managers were women whose husbands and sons were fighting. They found that harvesting farm produce was one thing, but assuring its proper distribution quite another. Before the war, boats had been used to transport crops as well as to supply the planter and his family with essentials such as ice and the daily paper; these could no longer function, due to Northern blockades.

In the years following Knox's death, Davis paid little attention to politics, despite Joseph's suggestion that he become involved. But this indifference to the political scene was soon to change. Jefferson realized that he could not isolate himself forever from the world, and so decided to visit an old friend, George W. Jones, a congressman from Michigan. In Washington, Jefferson met the politicians of the day, including Franklin Pierce, the representative from New Hampshire who later became President; the two became fast friends. This brief time spent in Washington had a great effect on Davis's career: in 1844, two years later, he ran for Congress, but lost the election because his district in Mississippi was Whig, not Democratic.

During that election year Miss Varina Howell was invited by Joseph to his plantation; she was the daughter of his intimate friend William Burr Howell. A handsome, clever girl, Varina had appealing dark eyes that contrasted with her mouth, which was full-lipped but pouting, giving her a haughty and slightly cruel look. Jefferson was attracted to her at once.

Of English and Welsh ancestry, Varina came from Natchez, Mississippi. Born in 1827, she was the granddaughter of Governor Richard Howell of New Jersey, and had been raised in comfortable surroundings. Moreover, having received a good

education, even at seventeen Varina was a brilliant conversa-
tionalist.

Upon meeting Jefferson, who was far older than she,
she wrote to her mother: "He impresses me as a remarkable,
kind man, but of uncertain temper, and has a way of taking for
granted that everybody agrees with him . . . which offends me
. . . yet he has a winning manner . . . the fact is, he is the kind
of man I should expect to rescue one from a mad dog at any
risk, but to insist on a stoical indifference to the fight afterward. I do not think I shall ever like him as I do his brother
Joe. Would you believe it, he is refined and cultivated, and yet
he is a Democrat!" (A typical Whig, Varina considered herself
socially superior to any Democrat.)

After a few weeks at the plantation, during which Varina
became attached to Jefferson Davis, she appeared one day not
wearing her heirloom brooch—her way of showing that she had
cast aside her family moorings. From this sign Jefferson
guessed that he might win her, and he guessed right. After a
somewhat stormy courtship they were married in 1845—ten
years after the death of his first wife—and made their home at
Brierfield. Varina was delighted with the funny house Jefferson
had designed, and teased him about the enormous fireplaces,
"looking as though they had been built in Queen Elizabeth's
time to roast sheep whole."

Immediately after the wedding the couple went to the plantation of Jefferson's sister Anna, where Knox had died; Davis
visited her grave—a natural act, but one wonders about Varina's reaction. Yet it was here, as she wrote in her memoir,
that she came to know intimately the man she had married.
"Mr. Davis was inclined to satire, and in his younger days in-
dulged in this propensity, never cruelly, but often to his own
injury. His sense of the ludicrous was intense, his powers of
observation were close, and his memory was phenomenal. He

Jefferson Davis's second wife, Varina Howell, at 18

seldom forgot a face, name or circumstance.... He was so consistent that he could not understand the incongruities of others.... He was excitable."

At Brierfield the newly married couple led a quiet life. Jefferson Davis was a great reader who liked not only sentimental poetry but also the works of John Locke, Adam Smith, Prescott, Gibbon, and Hume. He devoured Walter Scott's novels, and in odd moments would read up on military tactics. Living the life of a scholar, he was even so a man of action as well as a dreamer. Although not basically ambitious, he needed to achieve excellence in everything he undertook. His character was complex; Hudson Strode, in an introduction to *Jefferson Davis, Private Letters,* observes that they "give off further glints of the rainbow intangibility of [his] personality."

Plantation life meant hard work, yet it was luxurious. Governor John Quitman, a frequent visitor to Joseph's place, Hurricane, told how a guest was treated: "Your coffee in the morning before sunrise, little stews and soporifics at night, and warm footbaths if you have a cold. Bouquets of fresh flowers in your room. A horse and saddle at your disposal. Everything free and easy and cheerful and cordial."

Before Davis and Varina had celebrated their first anniversary, he was invited by the Mississippi Democratic leaders to run as representative-at-large in Congress. This time he won. "It was a singular coincidence," wrote Eckenrode, "that the leaders of the secession cause appeared in politics at the very moment of the issue that made secession inevitable," namely, the annexation of Texas, which brought up the agitating question of whether or not slavery should be permitted in that territory.

In his acceptance speech Davis told his constituents that he favored low tariffs, sound currency, the annexation of Texas, and a strict construction of the Constitution. Although he never enjoyed public speaking, the speech was a success; at the last minute Davis had discarded his prepared text and spoken off the cuff. "From that day forth," wrote Varina Davis in her memoir, "no speech [of his] was ever written for delivery." He became a splendid orator with a fine, modulated voice. Davis's words had a powerful impact on Senator John Calhoun, who predicted that his successor as leader of the South would be the young scholar-planter Jefferson Davis.

When Davis took his seat in the House of Representatives in 1845, he was thirty-seven. He had not spent as much as five dollars in campaigning. Varina later wrote that, as her husband entered his Congressional career, "he visited very little, studied until two or three o'clock in the morning, and, with my assistance, did all his writing, franking documents, letters, etc."

In the course of a discussion about General Zachary Taylor,

Davis's plantation home, Brierfield

Congressman Andrew Johnson (who later became President) took offense when Davis asked a rhetorical question as to whether a blacksmith or a tailor serving as a soldier could have fought the Mexican army as well as the trained officers and soldiers in Taylor's army. Johnson, a former tailor, heaped scorn upon the "illegitimate, swaggering, bastard aristocracy," of which he declared Davis was a member. The latter disavowed any intended slight, which should have satisfied Johnson but did not. From that time on, throughout the Civil War and its aftermath, he hated Jefferson Davis.

In one of his early speeches Davis urged compromise with England in the explosive Oregon boundary dispute. A few months later he was appointed to a Congressional committee to judge charges against Daniel Webster about his use of funds when Secretary of State under President Tyler (a resolution condemning Webster had been passed by the House, 136 to 28). Davis took a leading part in writing the committee report which exonerated Webster, although he observed, "No one would deprecate Webster's policy more than I do."

Davis now turned his attention to personal affairs. He wished to make his will, but could not leave Brierfield entirely to his wife, since Joseph had not deeded the property to him. Joseph in fact forced Jefferson to bequeath the plantation in equal shares to Varina and to his sisters. Varina was indignant, as was her husband. The brothers were not reconciled until the outbreak of the Civil War. Varina remained obdurate; "In 1861 my husband forgave his brother Joseph—I never did."

Varina was a fascinating person: emotional, puritanical, proud, generous—a woman of strong prejudices and powerful personality. Fiercely loyal, she was also jealously possessive, demanding evident appreciation of her affection. Although not by nature unkind, she sometimes hurt people with her barbed wit. Yet no one was better company than Varina, who had a lively sense of the ridiculous and loved a good laugh. Even in childhood, though, she had been moody and willful. Aware of her faults, she had warned Jefferson of her unstable character.

Her husband understood her. When the two became engaged, Jefferson had been calm and reassuring, telling her in a letter: "Some day I hope it will be mine always to be with you and then I shall possess increased powers to allay your nervous excitement. Until then may God and your good sense preserve you." He fulfilled this promise, although temperamental himself. Varina became strong and steady; consequently she had great influence on her husband, not only at home but also in political affairs. Usually he followed her advice, while maintaining his male dominance.

The many extant letters between Davis and Varina record a very close and lasting union between these two people of unusual intelligence who were temperamentally poles apart: she excitable and wayward, and he, with occasional lapses, self-controlled.

Before the outbreak of the war with Mexico in 1846, Jefferson and Zachary Taylor had become reconciled. Davis had resigned from Congress in order to enlist, and was selected to command the Mississippi Rifles, a volunteer regiment. It was equipped with special carbines which Davis obtained for his unit. When they joined Taylor's army, the Rifles were considered the best-trained of any outfit in it.

After the Americans had occupied the town of Saltillo, and the Mexican general offered to negotiate, General Taylor accepted. Taylor then named Jefferson Davis over several higher-ranking officers as one of three commissioners to take part in the peace talks. By then Davis had proved his ability as a military leader, and his men were devoted to him despite his strictness as a disciplinarian. His young brother-in-law, an officer serving under Davis, wrote from camp near Monterrey: "If the time of our regiment expires and our colonel even then thinks we could be useful, there is not a man in his regiment who would not sacrifice his life to obey him, so much has his gallant conduct raised him in their estimation. The degree of power his coolness, courage and discretion have acquired for him in the army generally would hardly be believed at home."

Ironically, it was precisely because "Old Rough and Ready" Zachary Taylor had conducted such a successful military campaign that Polk's Administration turned against him. The Democrats feared that the victorious Whig commander might be nominated for the Presidency (as indeed he was). Accordingly, in November, 1846, the Administration named Winfield Scott—another Whig, later dubbed "Old Fuss and Feathers" —to command the operation to capture Vera Cruz.

On February 22, 1847, Santa Anna attacked Taylor's left at Buena Vista with 20,000 men. Taylor had but 5,400, and when a regiment of American volunteers had been put to flight, the Mississippi Rifles were ordered forward. Davis, although badly wounded in one foot, advanced with his regiment to within eighty to a hundred yards from the enemy and, after two or three volleys, scattered the Mexican troops with the help of the artillery commanded by Captain William Tecumseh Sherman. (It is notable that almost every general of consequence in the Civil War served in Mexico.)

During this battle a group of Indiana soldiers was stationed by Davis on the brink of a ravine along the right flank of the Mississippi Rifles, forming a V, a new tactic that drew praise from the Duke of Wellington. Davis's stand had saved the day, and he was acclaimed nationwide.

Rightly so, for he had displayed brilliant tactics and shown outstanding military ability as well as courage. Yet Buena

Vista was a relatively minor battle, so that the young colonel should not have assumed, as he did, that he was expert as a tactician and strategist. This assumption led to overconfidence when Davis was called upon to direct the military effort of the Confederacy.

When General Taylor congratulated the wounded Davis, he said to a friend, "My daughter was a better judge of character than I."

Jefferson's wound kept him on crutches for more than twelve months. Though he must have been pleased when President Polk commissioned him a brigadier general of volunteers, he nevertheless declined the commission, feeling that only the State of Mississippi had the authority to grant it.

3

*Senator–Prelude
to Conflict
1847-1861*

In 1847 Governor Brown of Mississippi named Davis to replace U.S. Senator Jesse Spaight, recently deceased. Thus far
Jefferson Davis's ascent of the ladder of power had been easy,
and one wonders whether he might have become a more effective political leader had he been obliged to face serious
setbacks and disappointments early in life. In Allen Tate's
opinion, "he could not manage men, and he was too great a
character to let men manage him: that is the tragedy of his
career" (*Jefferson Davis: His Rise and Fall*).

The fact is, Davis lacked tact; in spite of his charming
manner he was unbending. Had he been through the hard
schooling of courthouse and statehouse politics, he might have
learned better how to handle voters and to lead them. He
would have understood that the successful political leader
must adjust himself to the frailties and eccentricities of his
supporters.

During the early days of the Mexican War, Davis's political
associates, Robert Barnwell Rhett, Leroy Pope Walker, and
William L. Yancey, had urged President Polk to annex all of
Mexico, threatening that their states might secede unless

Southerners were allowed to import slaves into the new territory. Massachusetts also had been ready to secede, opposing the war with Mexico because it feared that Mexico would become a slave territory. A few years later, however, Massachusetts and the other Northern states repudiated this extreme conception of state sovereignty, having then no reason to abandon the Union.

In 1848 the Whigs nominated Zachary Taylor for President, and the Democrats, Lewis Cass. Torn between loyalty to the Democrats and his personal attachment to Taylor, Jefferson Davis remained loyal to his party's nominee but did not campaign for him. And when the Democrats attacked Taylor, Davis came out strongly in his defense.

The Wilmot Proviso was introduced to Congress in 1847. It stated that in any territory acquired from Mexico, slavery must be barred. Though the Proviso failed to become a law by a slim margin, it stirred up a storm in the South, so that to many war seemed inevitable. It is significant that at this time, thirteen years before the outbreak of the Civil War, Davis wrote a public letter to the South: "Let us get together and build manufactures, enter upon industrial pursuits and prepare for our own self-sustenance." The South gave no attention to this advice, and when fighting the North paid dearly for its neglect.

In Washington, Davis shared lodgings with Senator Henry S. Foote of Mississippi and other Southern expansionists; the brash Foote had few friends in or out of Congress, and disliked Davis. On Christmas day of 1847, Davis and Foote got into a discreditable brawl in a Washington boardinghouse during which Davis swung his crutch and knocked off his adversary's wig. Thereupon Foote challenged Davis to a duel, which was averted by the persuasions of Varina and Howell

Cobb, Speaker of the House of Representatives. In 1851 Davis resigned from the Senate to run against Foote for governor of Mississippi; Foote won, much to Davis's humiliation. However, Foote's margin of victory was so small that Davis enthusiasts were already promoting him as a Presidential possibility.

A year before, the Clay Compromise, based on an earlier compromise evolved by Davis, had been debated in Congress. The subsequent Crittenden Compromise, which would have recognized slavery in territories south of 36° 30', was rejected by Henry Clay and Daniel Webster, and Davis himself opposed it after Lincoln's election. There could then be no halfway solution of the slavery question. "Slavery and the return of fugitive slaves are sacred matters and for this holy purpose the Revolutionary founding fathers met in Council," he observed. Unlike Calhoun, Davis did not believe that slavery was a permanent institution, but he felt that emancipation could not be attained for several generations.

In Davis's speeches and letters there is nothing to show that he was aware of the depth of Northern feeling about slavery. He thought that the Northern politicians' agitation against slavery was motivated by their struggle for sectional power. Though he stressed the fact that New Englanders had brought the slaves from Africa, he never made the most obvious criticism of the North: that in its factories women and children were cruelly exploited.

Davis opposed Henry Clay's and Stephen A. Douglas's slavery compromise measures of 1850, which were generally popular throughout the country; nevertheless, he retained his influence in the Democratic Party in both North and South. In 1852 the Democratic convention chose him for Vice President.

Jefferson remained in Washington as Mississippi's senator

for six years, until 1853, when President Pierce appointed him Secretary of War. In that capacity he engineered the Gadsden Purchase, whereby the United States bought 30,000 square miles of land from Mexico for $10 million. Active, energetic, inventive, Davis came to dominate the Cabinet. He kept an eye on his alma mater, West Point, of which Robert E. Lee was now superintendent (though too kind-hearted to maintain necessary discipline), for Davis was determined to make the academy outstanding. In addition, Davis increased the regular army from eleven to sixteen thousand men, and explored possible rail connections between the Mississippi valley and the Pacific—a development unpopular in the South. He was probably the best Secretary of War the country ever had.

In those days Varina sometimes became impatient with her husband's indulgence. Once, when she was annoyed at his treatment of some half-demented fellow, he replied, "It is a dreadful fate to be distraught and friendless." And when this man was later committed to an asylum, Davis sent him his own stationery so he could indulge his compulsion to write to persons in high positions. He himself answered the man's notes.

By 1857, when Jefferson Davis re-entered the Senate, he was the most important representative from the South—surprisingly, since he had spent little time courting his constituents. Unfortunately, he had not learned to curb his temper, though he did admit, "I have an infirmity of which I am horribly ashamed: When I am aroused in a matter, I lose control of my feelings and become personal." His encounter with W. H. Bissell, a colonel in the Mexican War, was a case in point; when Bissell belittled Davis's role at Buena Vista, Davis challenged him to a duel, choosing muskets loaded with ball at fifteen paces. Fortunately, friends intervened and the encounter was called off. Another duel threatened when Senator Judah P. Benjamin and Davis clashed over an army bill. Benjamin felt insulted and challenged Davis, who tore up the document, saying: "I was all wrong and will apologize to Benjamin." That a senator should come close to dueling so often seems incredible today. But in the period before the Civil War gentlemen were continually challenging each other, and Jefferson Davis, despite his sensitivity and innate gentleness, was capable of violent and thoughtless conduct.

While Jefferson had been absorbed in his political career, tragedy had struck at home. In 1858 Varina, who was to bear seven children, lost her firstborn. Two years later, she was in labor and close to death. In the middle of a severe Washington winter, medical help was difficult to get. Senator William H. Seward saved her life—as well as that of her new son, Jefferson—by sending his horse and sleigh to fetch a doctor. Afterward, Seward often visited the sickroom, and so began an extraordinary friendship between the Davises and this Northerner, who was to become Lincoln's Secretary of State.

That winter, when Jefferson fell ill with laryngitis, losing his power of speech and, temporarily, the sight of his left eye, Seward sat almost daily at his bedside. During one of these visits Davis asked his visitor how he could make moving appeals privately for the Negro, and still believe all he said in public debates. "I do not," Seward replied. Surprised by this answer, Davis said, "But, Mr. Seward, do you never speak from conviction alone?" "Never," Seward responded. Then Jefferson raised his head and whispered: "As God is my judge, I never spoke from any other motive." Seward put his arm around his friend, saying, "I know you do not. I am always sure of it."

—————————

At the Democratic nominating convention which met at Charleston on April 23, 1860, the delegates from Alabama insisted upon a platform proposed by William L. Yancey of Georgia: an ironclad restatement of the demand for a slave code for the territories, which was much the same as the proslavery resolutions that Jefferson Davis would bring up in the Senate a little later. Yancey, a prominent political figure in the South, was known as a fire-eater. The Alabama delegates had been instructed to withdraw from the convention if their platform was not accepted, and were supported in this stand by the other cotton states.

Stephen A. Douglas, a prominent Northwesterner noted for his debates with Abraham Lincoln, found it impossible to accept the Alabama proposals. He had told the Senate a few months previously: "I tell you, gentlemen of the South, in all candor I do not believe a Democratic candidate can ever carry any one Democratic state of the North on the platform that it is the duty of the Federal government to force the people of a territory to have slavery if they do not want it."

When Yancey insisted upon the adoption of his platform, the convention burst into an uproar. "Delegates rose to their feet, waving their arms, yelling frantically for recognition, screaming like panthers, and gesticulating like monkeys," according to an editorial in the *Cincinnati Commercial* quoted by Bruce Catton in *The Coming Fury*.

The convention adjourned until the next day, April 30, when it voted to adopt the Douglas platform. At this point the delegations from eight Southern states calmly withdrew, sensing that this fissure in the Democratic Party presaged a far more serious one for the Union. The Douglas faction had won the day and had their platform, but at the expense of party unity. Yancey observed: "The pen of the historian was nibbed to write the story of a new revolution."

William E. Seward,
Secretary of State
under Lincoln and
a once close friend
of Jefferson Davis

Library of Congress

It looked as though Douglas would easily win the nomination, until Chairman Caleb Cushing ruled that the nominee would have to obtain the votes of two-thirds, not of the delegates in the hall, but of the total number originally accredited to the convention. On May 3 the Charleston convention adjourned in a deadlock, after fifty-seven ballots, and voted to reassemble at Baltimore in June. Meanwhile a convention of the eight dissenting Southern states called by Yancey also adjourned, to meet again in Richmond in the same month.

37

Chicago Historical Society

Abraham Lincoln in 1860

The nation and the press had followed the convention with growing concern, and the *New York Times* editorialized: "The Democratic Party is the last of the great national organizations to yield to the irrepressible conflict which slavery and freedom have been waging for control of the Federal government." Thoughtful Southerners like Jefferson Davis did not wish the split to be permanent, but they were in the minority.

Not long after the deadlock at Charleston, a friend asked Senator Alexander Stephens of Georgia: "What do you think

*Stephen A. Douglas,
Democratic anti-
slavery candidate*

Library of Congress

of matters now?" "Think of them?" repeated Stephens, "Why, that men will be cutting one another's throats in a little while. In less than twelve months we shall be in a war, and that the bloodiest in history."

On May 9 a number of politicians and distinguished citizens convened in Baltimore. Calling themselves delegates to the Constitutional Union Convention, they nominated John Bell of Tennessee, a middle-of-the-road Southerner. The Constitutional Union Party was strong in the border states; it stood for "the Constitution of the country, the union of the states and the enforcement of the laws."

In the same month the Republican convention met in Chicago. The Republicans had emerged in 1854 as a party opposed to the extension of slave territory. In the Presidential election two years later the Republicans had attracted over 1,300,000 voters. Their platform was skillfully drawn to win support from the East as well as the West, from both conservatives and radicals. It proposed a protective tariff, internal improvements (including a railroad to the Pacific), and—surprisingly, in view of Lincoln's Emancipation Proclamation in 1863—the right of each state to control its domestic institutions. At their convention Senator William H. Seward, backed by his campaign manager, Thurlow Weed, was the favored candidate; he led on the first two ballots. Then Abraham Lincoln, proposed by Judge David Davis of Illinois, began to pick up votes, mainly because Seward was considered an antislavery radical. The seemingly more moderate Lincoln won the nomination.

The pro-Douglas Democrats reassembled at Baltimore on June 18, and a power struggle immediately began between Jefferson Davis and Douglas. Could the former unite the party and win the nomination? The Massachusetts leaders were for Davis, as were the delegates from Pennsylvania, Mississippi, and Arkansas. But he was not elected. If he had been, the rank and file of Northern Democrats would have voted for Lincoln and made the latter's victory overwhelming rather than marginal. It was then the accepted theory in the North that Davis was the man out to split the Union; on the contrary, he was at this time opposing secession except in the last resort. Indeed, he was criticized in the South for having made a speech in Maine some months previously, and accused of seeking Northern votes.

Davis and Douglas were bound to clash, although if Davis had been less inflexible, a compromise would have been possible. They agreed on the legitimacy of slavery, but differed on the question of slavery in the territories, Douglas holding that the people of a territory could decide whether or not to allow it. Davis, on the other hand, took the position that only when a territory became a state could it make this decision. This tragic quarrel contributed greatly to the Southern rejection of Douglas, the single viable Democratic candidate in 1860.

As it became clear that Douglas would win the Democratic nomination, John Russell of Virginia rose to his feet and announced: "It has become my duty now, by direction of a large majority of the delegates from Virginia, respectfully to inform this body that it is inconsistent with their convictions of duty to participate longer in its [the convention's] deliberations." His statement was greeted with cheers, hisses, and angry voices calling for order. During the confusion most of the Virginia delegates walked out, along with others from the Carolinas and Tennessee. They were followed by the Maryland delegation, as well as scattered groups from some of the Northern states and the Pacific coast.

Meanwhile, having met in Richmond as planned, Yancey's anti-Douglas faction reconvened on June 28 in the hall of the Maryland Institute in Baltimore. In addition to representatives from the cotton states, there were sixteen delegates from Massachusetts, two from New York, and one each from Iowa and Vermont. The border states were well represented, and there were delegations from California and Oregon. John C. Breckinridge of Kentucky was nominated.

There were now four candidates in the field: Douglas, Breckinridge, Bell, and Lincoln. Davis endeavored to persuade the three Democratic candidates to resign and agree on a compromise candidate, but Douglas refused. So ended the most vitally important and confusing succession of nominating conventions in our history. Given the divisions among his opponents, Lincoln was inevitably elected. The electoral vote demonstrated the sectional character of the contest, in which Lincoln carried eighteen free and no slave states, while Breckinridge carried eleven slave and no free states.

Following the news of Lincoln's election, South Carolina seceded from the Union in December of 1860. Senator Andrew Johnson of Tennessee, the poor white who would succeed Lincoln as President, denounced this act: "Whoever fires on our flag or attacks our forts I pronounce a traitor and he should meet a traitor's doom!" Davis retaliated by calling Johnson a "degenerate son of the South unworthy to sit in the Senate." The die was cast: Davis argued before the Senate the Constitutional right of secession.

Lincoln took the news of South Carolina's secession calmly, but sent word to Seward not to agree to the Crittenden Compromise, which might have preserved the Union without resort to war. Commenting on Lincoln's attitude, William E. Dodd wrote in his *Jefferson Davis:* "The popularity of the greatest war President has made students of the subject overlook his responsibility for this momentous decision."

In November, 1860, Jefferson Davis had received a letter from Robert Barnwell Rhett, asking his views regarding the attitude of Mississippi if South Carolina seceded from the Union. To this, Davis replied that he doubted whether South Carolina ought to secede unless the other cotton states followed. But on the very day of Davis's reply, South Carolina's legislature called for a "Sovereignty Convention" to meet a week later. At this point Jefferson Davis received a summons from the governor of Mississippi to confer with him and with other Congressional representatives about passing an ordinance of secession or trying to hold South Carolina in check pending concerted action later.

Davis immediately opposed separate state action, and was against secession so long as any prospect of a peaceable arrangement remained. Nevertheless, he stated that he intended to stand by the decision of the majority. His political associates felt that Davis was "too slow," that "he lagged behind the general opinion of the people of the State as to the propriety of prompt secession." According to Senator Clay of Alabama, Davis "reluctantly and regretfully consented to it as a political necessity for the preservation of popular and state rights."

On December 14, Jefferson Davis attended a meeting of a group of senators and representatives of nine Southern states to discuss the organization of Southern Confederacy through separate state secession. He agreed with the purpose of this meeting.

On January 21, 1861, about a month after South Carolina's secession, excited crowds gathered in Washington to hear Jefferson Davis make his farewell address before the Senate. By this time four Southern states besides South Carolina had decided to quit the Union. In view of this, many felt that Davis was acting like a traitor by staying on in Washington; Republican Senator Trumbull even maintained that Davis remained in the capital only to conspire and spy. Actually, Davis had remained because he understood, better than most of his countrymen from the South, the dire consequences of secession and the need for time to weigh the situation. Hot-tempered though he often was, he realized this was no time for hasty decisions or hasty action, and therefore warned his Southern colleague Rhett to be cautious and avoid antagonizing the Northerners.

When Jefferson Davis rose to deliver his farewell address to the Senate he was ill, tortured by a migraine headache that had kept him in bed for a week. His doctor did not think him

Institute Hall at Charleston wher

all for secession was made in 1860

CHARLESTON

MERCURY

EXTRA:

Passed unanimously at 1.15 o'clock, P. M., December 20th, 1860.

AN ORDINANCE

To dissolve the Union between the State of South Carolina and other States united with her under the compact entitled " The Constitution of the United States of America."

We, the People of the State of South Carolina, in Convention assembled, do declare and ordain, and it is hereby declared and ordained,

That the Ordinance adopted by us in Convention, on the twenty-third day of May, in the year of our Lord one thousand seven hundred and eighty-eight, whereby the Constitution of the United States of America was ratified, and also, all Acts and parts of Acts of the General Assembly of this State, ratifying amendments of the said Constitution, are hereby repealed; and that the union now subsisting between South Carolina and other States, under the name of " The United States of America," is hereby dissolved.

THE

UNION

IS

DISSOLVED!

*Notice of South Carolina's secession
from the Union in 1860*

even able to go to the Senate, but Davis knew the moment had come when he must speak out. The Senate galleries were jammed when he arrived, and in the crush the ladies' crinolines collapsed like pricked balloons. According to an account Bruce Catton gives in *The Coming Fury,* "A few seconds he hesitated, standing perfectly erect, almost swayback, in the manner of statesmen ... of his time. He was faultlessly dressed in black broadcloth, wore a black silk handkerchief tied stockwise around his neck and a white stiff shirt and black satin waistcoat. Under his high cheek-bones lay deep hollows; these and the square jaws and protruding chin gave the whole face a look of extreme emaciation—and of iron will. A glance at this man would have revealed his possession of complete self-mastery. Looked at more closely, he might have seemed less harmonized than self-conquered; as if he had suppressed a certain instability of temperament by will alone, and then ignored it. One would have supposed that the man could understand people intellectually, by a comparison of their ideas with his own; but not emotionally."

Davis started with these words: "I rise, Mr. President, for the purpose of announcing to the Senate that I have satisfactory evidence that the State of Mississippi, by a solemn ordinance of her people in convention assembled, has declared her separation from the United States." In her memoir Varina Davis commented on this event: "We felt blood in the air."

"Under these circumstances, of course, my functions terminate here. . . . States are sovereign. There was a time when none denied it. I hope this time may come again. . . . I am sure I feel no hostility to you, Senators from the North," he said in closing, "I am sure there is not one of you, whatever sharp discussion there may have been between us, to whom I cannot now say, in the presence of my God, I wish you well. . . . Mr. President and Senators, having made the announcement which the occasion seemed to me to require, it only remains for me to bid you a final farewell."

His speech has been described by the historian Hudson Strode as "one of the most moving and eloquent in American history." His words were brave and strong; few who heard them knew the toll they had taken. He had done what he had to do.

Jefferson Davis wrote to a friend: "We have piped but they would not dance, and now the Devil may care." To former President Pierce he said: "Civil War has only horror for me, but whatever circumstances demand shall be met as a duty and I trust be so discharged that you will not be ashamed of our former connection or cease to be my friend."

That night Davis tossed and turned in pain, almost blind from neuralgia. During the following week he sent letters and telegrams to leaders in every Southern state, advising against quick or violent action.

When Davis walked out of the Senate to fulfill his appointment as major general of the army of Mississippi, the Union expired. Thereafter there could be only one choice: the Northern civilization or the Southern. In the words of Allen Tate, "It would never be the same again; he was the last of the Senate giants."

After Jefferson Davis had taken leave of the Senate, his luck turned. Although he directed the Southern war effort as well as any man could, he had to face quarrels with the Southern politicians, with his generals, and with his people.

In the 1850s the South was rich. Even South Carolina, the least prosperous state in the Cotton Kingdom, was well ahead of Massachusetts in assessed value of property. Accordingly, had the War Between the States begun in 1850, before the

West became populated with immigrants unsympathetic to the South, the Confederacy would have had a better chance of winning. In the decade that followed, the North greatly expanded its industrial capacity. Jefferson Davis was well aware of this, and for many years had strongly urged the South to develop its manufacturing capability. As a military man he recognized Northern industrialization as the primary threat to Southern victory.

At the outbreak of the Civil War the population of the North far surpassed that of the South. And the strength of the North, financially as well as commercially, had by that time overshadowed the Confederacy. On the other hand, the Southerners were defending their homes and their way of life. But if the Old South in 1861 was a land of romantic fancy, it did not remain so for long. As the war imposed its harsh demands, the Confederacy became a place of regimented determination. Desperate men are a source of limitless strength; upon them Davis relied in the coming struggle.

Provisional President of the Confederacy 1861

The Southern convention that was held in Montgomery, Alabama, in early February, 1861, was still divided on the question of secession. In a preliminary vote it was rejected 54 to 46, though in the end it was approved 61 to 39. A constitution based upon the U.S. model having been adopted, the convention went on to elect a provisional President and Vice-President. Each of the six cotton states represented—the so-called "Gulf Squadron," composed of South Carolina, Georgia, Alabama, Mississippi, Florida, and Louisiana—had one vote. (Texas was about to secede but had not yet done so; the slave states were not yet united.)

Alexander H. Stephens, one of the candidates, was admired by blacks and whites alike; he was a small, frail man, but game as a fighting cock. An idealist, he had struggled in his youth to get an education, though handicapped by illness and poverty. Like Lincoln, who admired him greatly, he suffered from deep spells of melancholy. Once, after Stephens had spoken in Congress, Lincoln wrote: "I just take up my pen to say that Mr. Stephens of Georgia, a little, slim, pale-faced, consumptive man, has just concluded the very best speech of an hour's length I have ever heard." But Stephens was erratic, violent, and hypersensitive, and as such would become a thorn in Davis's side. He was elected provisional Vice-President of the Confederacy to serve under Davis, who was elected the provisional President.

In the *Charleston Mercury* Rhett criticized the convention for basically copying the U.S. Constitution and repudiating free trade. He further charged that "Jefferson Davis will exert all his powers to reunite the Confederacy with the Empire [the federal government]." Certainly there was plenty of dissent about Davis, and it is curious that the representatives decided to confer the office of President upon a man who had neither sought nor wanted it. He was elected because, as a reluctant secessionist, he appealed both to the conservative Virginians and to those Southerners who were still pro-Union. The convention lacked the conviction to choose an uncompromising radical.

"In 1861 few on either side doubted that [the new provisional President of the Confederacy] was abler than Lincoln . . . ," Samuel Eliot Morison has written. "Courage, patience and integrity were his; only perception and inner harmony were wanting to make him a great man." Jefferson Davis's weaknesses became apparent under the strains of war; he proved unwilling to delegate authority, he lacked tact and so antagonized his people, and he failed to prepare the electorate for the drastic war measures that had to be taken. In consequence, he was accused of dictatorship. Lincoln also was called a tyrant.

Davis had done nothing to advance his candidacy. He did not even attend the convention in Montgomery, where it was thought that the choice of President lay between Howell Cobb of Georgia and himself. But Cobb did not want the Presidency, and told supporters from his home state he hoped Davis would

*Alexander H. Stephens,
Vice President of the
Confederacy*

be chosen unanimously. Upon hearing this, the Georgia delegates next considered Robert Toombs, a former U.S. senator, but long discussion ended in a stalemate. Had the delegates agreed on Toombs, he would probably have made a popular President, for he was well-liked in the South. An outspoken, hard-driving man, and often profane, Toombs weakened his chances by his addiction to alcohol.

So it was that Davis, at Brierfield, received a telegram from Montgomery dated February 9, 1861:

> "Sir: We are directed to inform you that you are this day unanimously elected President of the Provisional Govern-

*Robert Toombs,
Secretary of State
of the Confederacy*

Library of Congress

ment of the Confederate States of America, and to request you to come to Montgomery immediately. We send you also a special messenger. Do not wait for him. R. Toombs, R. Barnwell Rhett, Jackson Morton."

When he received the notification, Davis exclaimed: "Oh God, spare me this responsibility," then added, "I would love to head the army." He was in the garden with Varina and reacted with a stricken look. After a moment of hesitation, he said: "The trial was too great and the result too doubtful to justify one in declining any post to which he was assigned, and therefore I accepted." Jefferson Davis fully realized that

Lincoln was inheriting a government established for eighty years, with fifty to a hundred times more manufactures than the South had, whereas he was launching a fledgling nation.

As the President-elect journeyed to the new capital, having left Varina at Brierfield until he could find a suitable home in Montgomery, not one person in a hundred thought that serious trouble lay ahead. Davis told the crowds welcoming him along the way to prepare for a long, hard war, but while he spoke well and his arguments were convincing, most of his supporters refused to believe him.

Davis reached Montgomery on February 16 and addressed a welcoming crowd at the Exchange Hotel. William L. Yancey stood at his side and, responding to the cheers, declared that at last the South had found "the statesman, the soldier and the patriot. The man and the hour have met."

Entering the Senate hall, Davis found himself beside Vice-President Stephens and Rhett. These two were to hound him unmercifully, Stephens for his usurping power from the people with which to wage the war, Rhett for his not fighting it aggressively enough.

On February 18, Jefferson Davis was formally inaugurated. He stood on a platform in front of the portico of the Alabama state capitol, as ten thousand people crowded round to see him. When the Presidential party reached the platform Howell Cobb, President of the Confederate Congress, administered the oath of office in a breathless silence during which Davis's "So help me God" rang out clear. Moved by this, the correspondent for the *New York Herald* wrote: "God does not permit evil to be done with such earnest solemnity, such all-pervading trust in His Providence, as was exhibited by the whole people on that day." Reaction abroad was also favorable (especially in England), and Davis himself could soon note

*William L. Yancey,
Confederate
commissioner
and Senator*

The New-York Historical Society

in the papers the contrast between his own triumphant arrival in Montgomery and Lincoln's stealthy entrance into Washington with two heavily armed companions.

Davis's acceptance speech, which made a favorable impression throughout the South and was reprinted in full in the *London Times,* was a plea for peace; it foreshadowed the defensive policy of his Administration in the opening phase of the coming war. In a letter to Varina dated February 20, he wrote: "I was inaugurated on Monday.... The audience was large and brilliant. Upon my weary heart was showered smiles, plaudits, and flowers, but beyond them, I saw troubles and

*Howell Cobb,
President of
the Confederate
Congress*

thorns innumerable. We are without machinery, without means, and threatened by a powerful opposition; but I do not despond, and will not shrink from the task imposed on me."

Great forces were about to be unleashed: violent nationalism at home, and abroad the intransigence of English millworkers dependent on cotton but opposed to Southern slavery. On the other hand the British upper class, including Queen Victoria, stood solidly behind the South, which was making the last stand for an agrarian society based on class rule; also, they wished America to be permanently divided.

Jefferson Davis immediately set to work trying to patch up the differences which divided the country. A week before Lincoln's inauguration on March 4, 1861, Davis appointed a commission to go to Washington and discuss possible peace terms with the new President.

Davis's Cabinet was adequate, but would have been better had he not followed the tradition of apportioning the offices evenly among the states. On the whole the Cabinet represented the conservative element, with the exception of Robert Toombs. All the appointees had been Unionists at one time or another, and two had opposed secession until their own states seceded. None was on intimate terms with the President. Commenting upon these appointments, Bruce Catton observes in *The Coming Fury*, "The executive would be Jefferson Davis and no one else."

The new President named Christopher G. Memminger, a man of superior intellect, as Secretary of the Treasury. Memminger would try to put the Confederacy on a sound financial basis through the sale of bonds and adequate taxation, but Congress resisted such taxation and the people had a deep aversion to it.

Robert Toombs, able, radical, eloquent, and colorful, was Secretary of State. He would have filled this position well, had he not felt that the President was monitoring him too closely. As it was, Toombs joined with Stephens in opposing the President, calling him "a fool and utterly incompetent." Toombs was considered in the South a "liquor-guzzling, throat-whiskered Georgian."

Leroy Pope Walker was Secretary of War: a decent, well-meaning man, but sickly and ineffective.

Judah P. Benjamin, Davis's old enemy in the U.S. Senate, became Attorney General. A highly competent Jewish Southerner, he later became Secretary of War, then of State, and proved to be the ablest man in the Cabinet. Though he did not

Judah P. Benjamin, Attorney General and Secretary of War and State of the Confederacy

Library of Congress

always agree with the President, he could dissent without giving offense.

Stephen R. Mallory, the Secretary of the Navy, was an excellent man unappreciated by Davis, who belittled his navy. Created from nothing, the Confederate navy astounded the world. It demonstrated the power of ironclad ships, introduced the underwater torpedo to modern warfare, and launched a successful submarine* (propelled by a screw worked by eight

---

* It was not the first submarine. According to a printed U.S. Navy statement exhibited at Pearl Harbor in 1977, a submarine designed by Ezra Lee, the *American Turtle,* attacked a British ship in New York harbor in 1776.

men), successful in that it destroyed an enemy ironclad, although its crew drowned when the submarine sank.

Finally, John H. Reagan was named Postmaster General. Reagan was from Texas, the seventh state to join the Confederacy. He was a competent official and, along with Mallory, the only cabinet member to retain his post throughout the war.

The Davises moved to a plain two-story frame house in Montgomery, where Varina entertained frequently and made useful political contacts. However, despite her vivacity and cheerful nature, she was not a social success in the beginning, because "refined" Alabama ladies said she was not a Southerner. First called "a Western woman," then a Western squaw, she was also dubbed "mullatto-ish" because of her tawny complexion. People criticized her for being bookish, coarse, brutal, and overly assertive, and even remarked snidely that she had once done her own housework. In spite of such petty sniping, Varina Davis kept up a good front. Her courageous stand did much to maintain her husband's morale, so that he leaned upon her more and more.

The Davises enjoyed a particularly happy family life. Jefferson had a special way with children, though perhaps he was overindulgent. His eldest daughter, Maggie, once said, "I wish I could see my father, he would let me be bad."

The President was so overworked that he could not take much part in social life, but his office was open to everyone, and when he had time to entertain, he was extremely gracious to his guests. But the cares of his office drained him; according to a British reporter, the expression on his face was anxious, and he had a very haggard, pain-drawn look.

Davis had expected the European countries to recognize the Confederacy and help its war effort, and with good reason—

Stephen R. Mallory, Secretary of the Confederate Navy

particularly in the case of England, which obtained from the South 80 percent of her cotton supply. In 1860 the South's cotton exports were huge: four and a half million people, mostly foreigners, were dependent on the industry.

The President appointed Yancey to head a commission to Europe; he probably should have chosen Benjamin instead, because Yancey was impetuous and proud. It is doubtful whether the commission would have been successful even then. The hope of obtaining foreign help was based on the implied threat of cutting off exports of cotton. Such thinking took no account of the fact that much of the 1860 crop had already been shipped abroad. Nor did Davis anticipate the decision of England and France to act together, which was fatal to the Southern cause.

Alexander Stephens urged the export of two million bales of cotton, in order to establish a credit of $500 million. Unfortunately, cotton in such quantity was not available, nor were there enough ships to carry it abroad. Under the circumstances, the new currency which was issued became almost worthless as the Civil War went on. Southern cotton was fated to be sold to Union merchants, confiscated by Union armies, and destroyed by retreating Confederates.

Davis also sent commissioners to Washington to see Lincoln. On March 11, 1861, they requested an interview with William H. Seward, Secretary of State. On the same day they dispatched a communication to the Department of State: "The Confederate States constitute an independent state, *de facto* and *de jure*, and possess a government perfect in all its parts; the Confederate government desires a peaceful solution of all pending disputes, wishes to make no demand not founded in simple justice and requests an immediate opportunity for the presentation of the credentials of its commissioners."

Two days later Mr. Justice Campbell, a friend of the commissioners, was assured that the Secretary of State was eager for peace, but desired to make no reply to the note for the present. Meanwhile attention had focused on Fort Sumter and other isolated federal posts guarding Charleston Harbor, which the North might reinforce or evacuate. Having spoken with Seward, Campbell now wrote to the commissioners: "I feel entire confidence that Fort Sumter will be evacuated in the next ten days."

Campbell's message was a strange one, since Lincoln had written on December 12, 1860: "Please present my respects to the General [Scott], and tell him, confidentially, I shall be obliged to him to be as well prepared as he can be to either hold or take the [Charleston] forts, as the case may require, at, or after, the inauguration."

Seward filed the commissioners' memorandum on March 15 with a note that, having consulted the President, he must decline "official intercourse" with them. They were not notified of this decision, however, and after waiting until March 18 for news, Davis wrote to South Carolina's Governor Pickens: "We have received nothing for several days from our commissioners, and I have not been of those who felt sanguine that the enemy would retire peaceably from your harbor."

In the meantime, since no word had come to confirm Seward's assurance that Sumter would be speedily evacuated by the federal forces, the Confederate commissioners approached Campbell once more. The judge agreed to talk again to Seward, who reassured him: "Faith as to Sumter fully kept—wait and see."

On March 20, 1861, however, Lincoln wrote Secretary of the Navy Gideon Welles regarding Sumter's relief: "I desire that an expedition to move by sea be got ready to sail as early as the 6th of April next." The memorandum designated the *Pocahontas*, the *Pawnee*, and a revenue cutter, and specified that five hundred men be ready at New York with the necessary arms.

The commissioners naturally concluded that they had been deceived. On April 9 they wrote to the U.S. Department of State, accusing the federal government of trickery and bad faith, adding: "Your refusal to entertain these overtures for a peaceful solution, the active naval and military preparations . . . are viewed by the undersigned, and can only be received by the world, as a declaration of war."

The moment of armed confrontation was approaching. On April 11, Colonel Chestnut and Captain S. D. Lee approached Fort Sumter and demanded its immediate surrender, stating that the Confederate States could "no longer delay taking possession of a fort which commanded one of their harbors." Major Anderson, senior officer of the fort, answered that a sense of responsibility made it impossible to comply at once, although "if you do not batter the fort to pieces about us, we will be starved out in a few days."

Since Anderson's reply offered the chance of avoiding bloodshed, General P. G. T. Beauregard, the Southern commander, passed it on to President Davis, who replied: "Do not desire needlessly to bombard Fort Sumter. . . . If Major Anderson will state the time at which . . . he will evacuate . . . you are authorized thus to avoid the effusion of blood. If this, or its equivalent, is refused, reduce the fort."

Beauregard immediately sent a second message to the fort; if Anderson would agree not to use his guns unless attacked, force might be avoided. The message was delivered at 12:25 A.M. on April 12. Three hours later Anderson replied: "I will evacuate . . . Fort Sumter by noon on the fifteenth instant, and I will not in the meantime open my fire against your forces unless compelled to do so by some hostile act against this fort or the flag of my government . . . should I not receive controlling instructions . . . or additional supplies." Since it was known in Charleston that the relief ships would arrive before April 15, this answer looked like a pretext for delay. The chance of taking Sumter without armed attack would then disappear.

Earlier that month Roger A. Pryor, a Virginian, had delivered a speech congratulating South Carolina on the annihilation of this "cursed union," adding: "I will tell your governor what will put Virginia in the Southern Confederacy in less than one hour by the Shrewsbury clock—'strike a blow'!" It is impossible to know how much the Charleston negotiators were influenced by their desire to have Virginia join the Confederacy. At all events they decided, without consulting President Davis or Beauregard, to send the following message to Major Anderson: "By authority of Brigadier General Beauregard, commanding the provisional forces of the Confederate States, we have the honor to notify you that he will open the fire of his batteries on Fort Sumter in one hour from this time."

At 4:00 A.M. on April 12, 1861, the lanyard of a cannon was pulled to fire on Fort Sumter. It is said that this first shot of the Civil War was fired by Edmund Ruffin, an elderly planter and an authority on soil chemistry, who was chosen for the assignment because for years he had been a leader among the radical secessionists. Those sharing his views had formed Committees of Correspondence similar to those organized by Samuel Adams before the American Revolution, and had also organized a society of minutemen. As Bruce Catton observes in *The Coming Fury,* "secession was the culmination of years of radical tactics and revolutionary propaganda."

Possession of Sumter was a cardinal point of Jefferson Davis's strategy as well as that of Lincoln. Pleasant A. Stovall, a statesman from Georgia, was opposed to firing on the fort. He wrote: "The firing on that fort will inaugurate a civil war

National Archives

*Edmund Ruffin, rumored to have fired
the first shot of the Civil War*

Confederate flag over Fort Sumter

National Archives

greater than any the world has yet seen. To do so at this time is suicide, murder, and will lose us every friend in the North. You will wantonly strike a hornet's nest which extends from mountains to ocean, and legions now quiet will swarm out and strike us to death. It is unnecessary; it puts us in the wrong; it is fatal." Stovall attributed this statement to Robert Toombs, of whom he wrote a biography, but it is highly doubtful that Toombs, a Southern fire-eater, would have made it.

Bombarded for thirty-four hours, Fort Sumter at last surrendered, without bloodshed. Its fall marked the start of the Civil War: while the Confederate flag flew over the fort, there could be no compromise. In both North and South, pent-up emotions were released, making a long, savage war unavoidable.

A little more than a fortnight after Sumter's surrender, William H. Russell, a correspondent of the *London Times,* visited the capital of the Confederacy. Though he felt that this people might wage a highly successful war, he could not sympathize with many of their customs. He found Montgomery as primitive, dull, and lifeless as a town in Russia. The widespread tobacco chewing appalled him, although the Southerners themselves—tall, lean, and rough—impressed him greatly. Russell considered the members of the Confederate Congress equally imposing; they looked to him like old-time Covenanters: big, earnest men inspired by strong faith. "They were like the men who first conceived the Great Rebellion which led to the independence of this wonderful country—so earnest, so grave, so sober and so vindictive." He agreed with Varina Davis, who wrote to a friend that the representatives in the Southern Congress "are the finest looking set of men I have ever seen collected together—grave, quiet and thoughtful with an air of refinement"—in contrast to the less impressive congressmen in

Washington. Russell judged this Southern Congress rightly, but he would have been even more impressed by the preceding provisional Congress. Unfortunately, with time the quality of the Southern congressmen deteriorated.

At this time Alexander Stephens made a significant speech at Savannah: "Many governments have been founded upon the principle of the subordination and serfdom of certain classes of the same race . . . our system commits no such violation of nature's laws. With us, all of the white race, however high or low, rich or poor, are equal in the eyes of the law. Not so with the Negro. Subordination is his place . . . in conformance with the ordinance of the Creator."

This statement, made by the man who had opposed secession, clearly established slavery as the foundation of the Confederate government, and let the Abolitionists convert a Constitutional controversy into an antislavery crusade. Seizing the opportunity, they interpreted the speech as though it had been an article in the Confederate Constitution. Despite the protests of Davis, thereafter the North strove—in the end successfully—to make Stephens's statement appear as the battle cry of the South.

Had Fort Sumter not been fired upon, what other cause would have led to war? It was not the issue of slavery, nor even the question of states' rights that was decisive. These were merely triggers that awoke Americans to the fact that, for nearly one hundred years, North and South had coexisted peaceably with little in common except one grandly ambivalent instrument, their Constitution, which told them they were free —which also meant, according to the Southern interpretation, free to go their own separate ways. In 1861, people in this country realized that their Constitution was out of date. Big as the country was, there was room for only one way of life, an issue that had to be decided on the battlefield.

Following the surrender of Fort Sumter, volunteering boomed in the North, where Lincoln called for 75,000 men to enlist for three months. Davis, being more aware of the magnitude of the coming conflict, and discounting the assumption in the South that the Confederate soldier was superior to the federal one, asked for 100,000 men for a twelve-month enlistment; three times that number volunteered.

On April 17, 1861, Virginia finally seceded. Within a few weeks North Carolina, Arkansas, and Tennessee followed. Virginia's hesitation probably cost the Confederacy the border states of Maryland and Kentucky, and possibly Missouri. Had Maryland seceded, the Union would have lost Washington; moreover, with the above-mentioned states on the side of the South, as well as southern Illinois and southern Indiana, which would have followed suit, the Confederacy might have won the war. Without these areas in the Southern camp, it was a closely fought conflict; with them, the Southern cause would have been substantially strengthened.

The Early
Victories
1861-1862

The atmosphere of Montgomery did not appeal to the Southern politicians and their wives; it was a small, shabby town of nine thousand inhabitants, of whom half were black. Eighteen years before the start of the Civil War, a team of oxen had drowned in one of the many deep mudholes that still existed in the city. Accordingly, the politicians started a successful agitation to move the capital to Richmond, Virginia, and at its next session the Congress decided on the change. Jefferson Davis is reported to have protested: it was a mistake, he thought, to have the capital on the frontier, requiring maximum protection without any offsetting advantage. Furthermore, because the Mississippi Valley was the real strategic center of the war, the move to Richmond would make it necessary to split the Confederate army between East and West.

But there was a valid reason for the move: in 1861 Richmond was the nearest thing to a manufacturing center in the South. Above all, in Richmond were the Tredegar Ironworks, the only established facility in the Confederacy for making large-scale machinery and heavy weapons. And the strategic disadvantage to the Confederacy of maintaining headquarters at Richmond was offset by the preoccupation of Northern strategists with the idea of "On to Richmond." For years this fixation impeded Union plans to place their troops in adequate numbers outside Virginia.

On his journey to Richmond, Davis received ovations, but the Virginians considered him an upstart: who was his grandfather, anyway? Thereafter, local ladies became indignant when Varina, arriving late at church one Sunday, found a plainly dressed woman seated in the President's pew, and waited impatiently for her to vacate it. The woman was Mrs. Robert E. Lee, and instantly those in nearby pews threw their doors open to her. Although the incident was regrettable, there had been no intention to humiliate the general's wife, a wise woman who, when the Civil War broke out, had exclaimed: "Both parties are wrong in this fratricidal war."

Davis's reception by the Richmond press was mostly adverse; the *Richmond Whig* and the *Richmond Inquirer* attacked him unmercifully. Also in opposition was the *Charleston Mercury*, controlled by Robert Barnwell Rhett, who had been mentioned as a candidate for the Confederate Presidency, so that there was even discussion in the Cabinet about purchasing a Richmond paper in order to secure some support for the Administration. A chorus of Davis attackers declared that Richmond had become more depraved after two years of war than Washington under the Buchanan Administration.

The *North Carolina Standard* and the *Montgomery Advertiser* first supported Davis, but as the fortunes of the Confederacy waned, they too became critical. Not all the press was "agin the government," however: the *Richmond Enquirer*, probably the best paper in the South, supported the President and his administration to the end of the war. Most Northern papers sided with the Lincoln Administration, but Davis declared that he had to endure more criticism from the Southern press than from the Northern.

National Archives

———————————————★————————————————

Jefferson Davis now turned meticulous attention to building up his army, which he concentrated in Virginia. At Manassas, thirty miles from the capital, the first important battle of the war, Bull Run, took place in July, 1861. At first it looked as though the rebels would be defeated, but an obscure, eccentric officer—a former West Pointer and professor at the Virginia Military Institute, in command of one of the brigades—regrouped his troops into an impenetrable barrier and saved the day. From that time on, this man, who developed into a general second only to Lee in ability, was called "Stonewall" Jackson.

After the victory Davis, abandoning his defensive stance, summoned his officers and gave orders to Generals Beauregard and Joseph Johnston to pursue the enemy. They pleaded that their troops were exhausted, that they lacked transportation. And so, according to a number of military authorities, the chance to take Washington with only 10,000 men was lost; in their view, a determined attack with forces which, man for man, were at this time superior to the Northerners, could even have won the war. However, Bruce Catton maintains that the Confederacy lost little by not pursuing the Union army because, in his opinion, Washington was not then open to sudden capture by the enemy. Whatever the truth, the battle of Bull Run had an important effect: it convinced the South that it would require years of effort to gain independence, and it converted a rebellion into a civil war.

At Bull Run the soldiers on both sides were untrained and in need of leadership. In this battle, more than in any of the war, much depended on the brigade and division commanders. General Sherman, later the conqueror of Atlanta, described Bull Run as one of the best planned, but one of the worst fought, battles in history. "Both armies were fairly defeated," he said, "and whichever stood fast, the other would have to run."

At Bull Run the Arkansas Greys—a cavalry regiment raised and equipped at the expense of a woman named Loretta Janetta Velasquez—fought alongside the Confederate forces. She took part, disguised as a man, and subsequently became a spy for the South.

In the weeks after the battle, Jefferson Davis devoted his energies to building up adequate stocks of food for his growing army. He did not always find dealing with his generals easy, and was forced to resort to diplomacy—a new stratagem for him, since he was not by nature of a conciliatory disposition.

The lull in hostilities following Bull Run let the North raise a large army; Lincoln asked Congress for 500,000 men and $400 million, and obtained both. George B. McClellan was placed in command of the forces assigned to capture Richmond. The appointment of the highly cautious McClellan was a mistake, although Jefferson Davis, when Secretary of War, considered McClellan the ablest officer in the army. The Union was in fact short of good generals, whereas in the Southern agricultural society young men, seeking an outdoor life, flocked to the excellent Southern military academies. One hundred and eighty-two Confederate general officers started their careers in the U.S. army; on the whole they were an able lot.

Jefferson Davis remained confident, although he had no offensive plans at this time. He had more than 100,000 men under arms, exclusive of home guards and militia; but weapons were scarce, as were supplies, and the shortages proved impossible to correct, given the lack of manufacturing facilities. While there were shortages in the North too in 1861, the problem was quickly solved once the Union became organized.

In August of 1861 President Davis appointed five full generals: Samuel Cooper, Albert Sidney Johnston, Robert E. Lee, Joseph E. Johnston, and P. G. T. Beauregard. The list was in

*Confederate General
P. G. T. Beauregard*

Library of Congress

*Confederate General
Joseph E. Johnston*

75

order of seniority, Cooper, the Adjutant General, was the oldest and Beauregard the youngest. Because the first three had won no battles, the friends of Joseph Johnston and Beauregard were indignant about the honor conferred on them. Johnston complained personally to Davis, claiming that his rank had been reduced; he felt that he should be the superior officer.

Beauregard, who was hoping to be elected permanent President of the Confederacy in place of Davis, was vitriolic. He too was nursing his wounds over Bull Run, feeling that he had been unjustly treated. In his report on the battle, submitted over three months after it had taken place, he stated that he had sent one of his staff officers to Davis with a plan to defeat the enemy at Bull Run and capture Washington, but that Davis had disapproved the plan. After all this was headlined in the press, Beauregard anticlimactically withdrew his charge. Joseph Johnston was drawn into the altercation because Davis asked him, as Beauregard's superior officer, to state whether or not Davis had obstructed pursuit of the enemy after Bull Run. Johnston was generous enough to exonerate the President.

The struggle between Beauregard and Joseph Johnston with Jefferson Davis continued throughout the war. Dissatisfied army officers and congressmen with grievances joined ranks behind their two military champions. Meanwhile Davis decided to replace the outwardly dashing Beauregard, who had fallen ill after Bull Run. Beauregard was glamorous, and saw himself as a second Napoleon, when actually he was only a fairly good general and certainly not a great one. Often he was overcautious, yet at the same time he made reckless plans. But basically he had the right idea: to destroy the army of the enemy.

Later that summer the seizure of J. M. Mason and John Slidell, the Confederate commissioners to England and France,

Union General George B. McClellan

who were traveling on the British packet *Trent,* created a sensation overseas. This daring act, for which Captain Charles Wilkes of the U.S.S. *San Jacinto* was responsible, caused the *London Morning Chronicle* to observe: "Abraham Lincoln, whose accession to power was generally welcomed on this side of the Atlantic, has proved himself a feeble, confused and little-minded mediocrity." A few months later Queen Victoria, commenting on the *Trent* affair, declared that the British lion could not be insulted with impunity. England sent a stiff note demanding surrender of the prisoners and disavowal of this act of seizure. She prepared for war and sent troops to Canada; there was even talk of blockading the federal navy. The situation had become so explosive that Washington's minister to London, Charles Francis Adams, was obliged to request an official dispatch from his government stating that the seizure of the commissioners had been unauthorized. The storm gradually subsided when Lincoln ordered the release of Mason and Slidell.

By the end of February, 1862, when Davis realized that his dream of European intervention was illusory—and that continuance of the war was highly profitable to Great Britain—he had the courage to change his policy completely. Against opposition from Vice-President Stephens, who continued to impede the military effort, he advocated compulsory military service and the passage of the first conscription act in American history. The draft was overdue, but Davis's assumption of centralized power conflicted with the states' rights principle for which the Southern states had seceded.

Roanoke Island, off the North Carolina coast, fell to the Union forces on February 8, 1862; eight days thereafter Fort Donelson in Kentucky surrendered to General Ulysses S. Grant, with the result that the ill-equipped Southern army of the able

General Albert Johnston had to evacuate Nashville, Tennessee. The news of Donelson's fall, where twelve thousand Southern soldiers were taken prisoner, shook the Confederacy. The defeat occurred in the month before Jefferson Davis was inaugurated as permanent President, and it gave his enemies the opportunity to voice bold criticism of him. Having been "the idol of the people," Davis became unpopular, and Stephens in particular opposed the Administration.

Another result of the Confederate reverses was Congress's demand that Judah P. Benjamin be removed as Secretary of War; Davis, however, defended him and appointed him Secretary of State right after the fall of Donelson. Benjamin was a remarkable man, of whom Varina Davis had once remarked: "Mr. Benjamin's courtesy in argument was like the salute of the duellist to his antagonist whom he intends to kill, if possible."

Born a British subject, he was both hated and loved in the Confederacy; in the U.S. Senate he had been popular on both sides of the house. Yet he offended the Confederate generals and was tactful only with Jefferson Davis—a good thing, since the President failed to relish advice strongly presented, and could not understand how anyone could differ with his opinion. Though he was a first-rate, hard-working administrator, as Secretary of State, Benjamin was sometimes mistaken. He remained convinced to the end that Europe would recognize and aid the Confederacy.

The North was superior to the South in numbers as well as in economic strength; moreover, Lincoln succeeded in centralizing the authority of his government—a goal that Davis could not achieve, because of the South's distrust of centralization. The Northern population rose to 22 million during the war, including 800,000 immigrants, half of whom served in the Union army. In contrast, the population of the Confederate States was 9 million, but 3.5 million were slaves who did not fight. This disproportion was less serious for the South than might be supposed, because during most of the war the Confederate armies were operating on short interior lines, while the Union had to fight an offensive war with long lines of communication.

In 1862 it was proposed that General Jackson's army in the Valley of Virginia be strengthened, so that he might undertake a vigorous offensive campaign against the North in Pennsylvania, even at the risk of having to abandon Richmond. On June 18, 1862, Lee pointed out in a dispatch to the President that, even if he used as many as 100,000 troops to resist a siege of Richmond, he might only prolong it and fail to save the capital.

Robert E. Lee was now appointed by Davis as his chief military adviser in Richmond, a daring move because Lee's recent military operations in Western Virginia had been unsuccessful. This decision by the commander-in-chief was probably his most important contribution to the Confederate cause. Nevertheless, the *Richmond Examiner* protested that Lee was a "book soldier," inept on the battlefield, and called him a coward because he had advised entrenchments. In contrast to this opinion the military memoirist Wolseley wrote of Lee as "one of the few men who ever seriously impressed and awed me, with their natural, their inherent greatness."

Jefferson Davis aroused opposition by insisting upon conscription, which he considered imperative in order to oppose the quickly augmenting armies of the North. In April, 1862, the Confederate Congress finally passed a law drafting ablebodied men between eighteen and thirty-five for three years. Protests came from various localities, especially from Georgia, where Robert Toombs, Stephens, and Governor Joseph E.

Brown led the opposition, denouncing conscription as unconstitutional. The law raised an anti-Davis clamor that was to continue to the end of the war. Professor Dodd has called this "a most important, if not the greatest, cause of the final collapse of the Confederacy."

In April 1862 things looked bleak: McClellan's picket line was but four miles from Richmond. The government archives were loaded for immediate removal and Varina, with her family, moved to Raleigh, North Carolina. The military situation took a turn for the worse when General George B. McClellan's large federal army began advancing on Richmond from the east, moving slowly up the peninsula between the York and James rivers.

There was little to block the Union's advance: General John B. Magruder, with only 10,000 men armed for the most part with "Quaker cannon"—logs painted black—was holding a fortified line at the tip of the peninsula, facing McClellan's 100,000 federals. Had McClellan not delayed, as was his habit, he could have crushed Magruder before the arrival of Joseph Johnston.

Obligated to remain in Richmond, Davis was out of touch with the West. The Mississippi had not been adequately fortified; on April 24, 1862, Flag Officer David G. Farragut bombarded the forts defending New Orleans, after which the South's greatest port was occupied by Union General Benjamin F. Butler. This was a disaster for the South, which lost the lower Chesapeake Bay in the same spring. These reverses were somewhat offset by the heroic struggle between the Confederate ironclad *Merrimac* in the bay, on the water route to Richmond, against the federal *Monitor*. The five-hour fight was the first naval battle in history between two ironclads, and ended in a draw.

After his defeats by Grant, Albert Johnston assembled an army at Corinth, Mississippi, with the plan to fall upon Grant before General Buell could join him. On April 6, 1862, he met Grant at nearby Shiloh in a furious battle where colonels fought like privates and privates led companies. Just as he had broken the center of Grant's line, Johnston was hit in an artery by a chance Minié ball; instead of having the wound attended to, he remained in the saddle and bled to death. Beauregard took his place, but the impetus of the Confederates had been lost, so that this extremely bloody battle ended inconclusively. After a two-day struggle the Southerners withdrew to Corinth.

Grant, who up to now had been certain that the rebel cause was doomed to early defeat, came to realize, as had Jefferson Davis after the First Battle of Bull Run, that the war would be long and bitter. In his memoirs he wrote: "I . . . believed that the Rebellion . . . would collapse suddenly and soon, if a decisive victory could be gained over any of its armies." After Shiloh he concluded that victory would come only "by complete conquest."

For Davis the death of Albert Johnston, his close friend whom he much admired as a military commander, was piercing; he had lost one of his three key generals, the other two being Lee and Jackson. At this low point Davis admitted in a letter to a friend, "I acknowledge the error of my attempt to defend all of the frontier, seacoast and inland, but will say in justification that if we had received the arms and munitions which we had good reason to expect, the attempt would have been successful."

The Minié ball that killed Albert Johnston was designed by a Frenchman. It changed the nature of war, increasing the maximum range of a rifle from one hundred yards to five hundred. The Minié expanded in the bore of the rifle and thus utilized to the full the powder gases forming behind it. With the killing zone five times as great, the defense became far more effective and the offense more hazardous. Neither Lee nor Grant understood the revolution marked by the Minié; indeed, it was not understood even as late as World War I.

Pondering his mistake of attempting to defend too much territory, Davis compared his reaction to criticism with that of his seven-year-old daughter, and wrote: "Maggie is a wise child. I wish I could learn just to let people alone who snap at me; in forbearance and charity to turn away from the cats as well as the snakes." He knew this flaw in his character, this inability to ignore criticism, but could not refrain from answering back.

Lincoln was as eager as Grant for final victory, but he had been less optimistic about the time needed, and even so had been disappointed by his generals. McClellan was proving a failure, and Lincoln likened sending troops to him to shovelling fleas across a barnyard; only half seem to arrive.

A Southern woman's exploit in the Shenandoah Valley brought some cheer to Richmond. In May, 1862, during the struggle for control of this crucial valley leading to the Northern heartland, Belle Boyd—the most sensational of the Confederate spies—ran across open fields exposed to the crossfire of both armies, and crawled along the hilltops, waving her sunbonnet until she came close to the Confederate lines. Here she succeeded in giving to General Stonewall Jackson the disposition of the Union troops—a vitally important message. A few days later Jackson wrote to her: "I thank you, for myself and for the Army, for the immense service you have rendered your country." (Later Belle survived two imprisonments, and ended by marrying a Union officer.)

Jackson's valley campaign was brilliantly successful. He

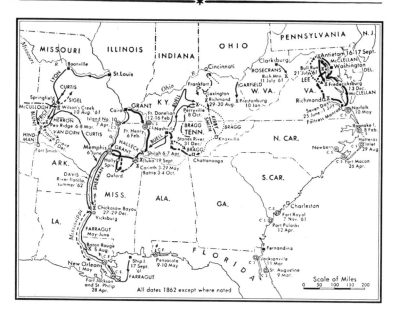

Areas of fighting in 1861–1862

routed federal forces two and a half times as large as his own, and on May 25 compelled them to retreat across the Potomac. The capture of the Shenandoah Valley provided the Confederacy with a vital source of food and fodder.

But the Confederate reverses in the West had given Rhett the opportunity to call Davis "conceited, wrong-headed, wranglesome, obstinate—a traitor." Suffering from migraine, Davis became increasingly frail. Having assumed too many duties, he found it difficult to direct the war effort effectively. If Lee had been made head of the Southern armies at this time, the Confederates might still have won.

In May the Southern forces under Joseph E. Johnston had withdrawn to the outskirts of Richmond. Jefferson Davis was dissatisfied with Johnston's movements and felt that the capital was in danger. On May 23, Davis and Lee visited Johnston near Mechanicsville, a village six miles from Richmond, but Johnston would tell them nothing definite. Two days later, the Union troops occupied Mechanicsville, from which they could see the church spires of the capital.

Following another visit from Lee, Johnston finally announced that he planned to attack McClellan's army, and on May 31 he advanced to a settlement known as Seven Pines. As soon as the President learned of the fighting, he and Lee rode out "in time to see a battle mismanaged"; the Confederate staff work was poor and the attack was not progressing. As darkness was beginning to fall, an excited messenger informed Davis that Johnston had been severely wounded. The President came upon the general being borne on a litter. When Davis spoke to him, Johnston opened his eyes, smiled, and gave him his hand. He said that he did not know how badly he was hurt, but feared a shell fragment had injured his spine.

Davis and Lee then rode back toward Richmond, apprehensive about the next day's fighting. Deep in thought, Davis turned to his companion, and said, "General Lee, I am assigning to you command of the army." This was a climactic moment, for it gave Robert E. Lee his chance to prove his genius as a fighting commander. When Davis reached his office, he wrote out an order making Lee commander of the Army of Northern Virginia.

That night the citizens of Richmond tossed in their beds with apprehension; the city was filled with wounded soldiers. Warehouses were converted into hospitals and, to give comfort to the wounded, householders fetched from their cellars their best port and Madeira. At noon Jefferson Davis started out for the battlefield through scenes of suffering; arriving, he conferred with Lee. The battle around Seven Pines was still going on and the Confederates were having a difficult time. The fight ended indecisively, but the Southerners soon recovered the initiative and forced the enemy to withdraw from Richmond.

In the Seven Days' Campaign that followed (June 26–July 2, 1862), Lee's plan was overly elaborate, his staff work bad, and his troop movements poorly coordinated. For all that, he saved Richmond and forced McClellan to retreat, though the federal army was by no means destroyed. The failure of the Peninsular Campaign led to McClellan's recall to Washington, whence he was ordered to unite with General John Pope, whom Lincoln had appointed commander of the newly created Army of Virginia.

Meanwhile, Lee's promotion had been received with little enthusiasm by the troops, who admired Johnston. It seemed that no one in the Confederacy agreed with Jefferson Davis that Robert E. Lee had great potentialities, both as a commander and as an organizer. And few thought that this gentle-mannered soldier was a man who would take daring chances. In point of fact Lee, together with other generals under his command, had to be restrained from leading charges. Southern commanders felt that they should set an example for the other officers, and as a result suffered enormous attrition—all in the name of Southern chivalry.

Following the succession of Southern defeats in the West, the Congress in Richmond voted to relieve the President of his post as commander-in-chief and to appoint Lee to that office. The resolution was vetoed by Davis, who soon afterward appointed Lee the first military officer in the Confederacy. Rhett, along with Governor Brown of Georgia and Stephens, joined forces to oppose Davis, pursuing a course that hastened the collapse of the Confederacy.

Lee left Richmond for the field of battle declaring that Jefferson Davis was "the best military adviser that I have ever consulted." The President then appointed James A. Sedden, a shrewd lawyer, but a highly strung man like himself, to the post of Secretary of War. Sedden lacked military experience, but he had plenty of military sense and was wise enough not to cross Davis. General Braxton Bragg also retained his command in the West because he never attempted to oppose the President. Davis's support of Bragg as a field general was one of his few mistakes in choosing commanders although, like Lincoln, he sometimes interfered with their operations in the field. (By way of contrast, Lincoln's appointments of generals were often badly mistaken, especially during the first years of the war.)

By mid-1862 the Confederate military situation had taken a distinct turn for the better. Despite the serious Confederate reverses in the West, McClellan had been driven from Richmond, following which Lee attacked John Pope and on August 26, 1862, in the Second Battle of Bull Run, smashed him in an action that has been called Napoleonic in conception.

The North was discouraged. In this emergency Lincoln, contrary to the advice of his Cabinet, turned to McClellan to save his capital by once more taking command of the Army of the Potomac. Lincoln, though discouraged by "Little Mac's" previous military failures, counted upon his dynamic appeal to rally the disheartened Union troops. When the President's decision was announced, the cheering among the soldiers for their adored commander was heartfelt and vociferous.

What was the secret of McClellan's magic? This ambitious, vain, but personally brave man had not achieved a single important victory, and he had failed to follow the enemy when the advantage was on his side. Yet McClellan's troops idolized this consummate drillmaster who had a genius for organization, and who could hardly bear to take his beloved soldiers into bloody attack. McClellan hid his overwhelming self-confidence behind a curtain of charm, and this, perhaps, was the secret of

Library of Congress

*Confederate General
Braxton Bragg*

his magic. Lincoln saw through McClellan but believed that, with his back against the wall as at this moment, he would acquit himself well in a defensive action.

During this time Confederate hopes were high and the fortunes of Jefferson Davis reached their peak. Victory was in sight and, although Davis did not know it, England and France now came as close to intervention as they ever would.

Although the South's military situation had much improved during 1862, the wounded packed the halls, drawing rooms, and porches of the houses in Richmond. Young belles worked in the hospital wards all day only to change, at sundown, into ball gowns and dance with the lightly wounded soldiers until dawn.

Southerners were financially pressed. The price of food had risen alarmingly: in 1863 a barrel of flour sold in the street for

$115; for $75 one could buy only a modest quantity of tea and sugar, while a spool of thread cost $4. Twenty dollars for five dozen eggs was considered a fair price. Southern currency had become worthless.

As the months wore on there were many shortages which Southern women had to deal with, but they were quick to discover how to make starch from sweet potatoes and green corn, and that boiling the roots of the buckeye with flannel produced an acceptable substitute for soap.

While mustard was found to be a palatable "green," so were wild garlic, sassafras, sorrel, pokeweed, and pepper grass. None of these, however, could stem the epidemic of scurvy that broke out, and the price of medicines, especially quinine, soared. The absence of sufficient chloroform, and of trained nurses to help the overworked surgeons, were also pressing problems; many Confederate soldiers died when even mild wounds became gangrenous. Doctors learned to treat lung infections with a syrup of mullein leaves and cherry bark, but it was not very effective. Men suffering from dysentery, which was widespread, were given a cordial, or persimmons and blackberry roots.

Soon women were obliged to find substitutes for dyes hitherto imported from the North: they discovered that pine-tree-root extract produced an acceptable shade of garnet; myrtle, a soft gray; and hickory bark, a bright green. The mordants used to set these dyes included old horseshoes, clamps, hinges, and rusty nails.

Because of the inadequate supply of metal in the South, soldiers lacked ammunition. Accordingly, the large bells of many Mississippi plantations were given to the Confederate army to be converted into cannons. Congregations voted to donate their church bells and, when these proved insufficient, many women offered the weights from their window sashes.

It was almost impossible to purchase paper, pens, and ink at any price. The outmoded goose quill returned to fashion, and people wrote on the reverse side of wall-paper, using the crimson sap of oak galls for ink.

"Confederate candles"—bottles sporting circles of rope dipped in tallow—allowed enterprising Southern women to knit after sundown, though the dim light they provided was difficult to read by. Stays remained one of the few essentials of life for which no replacement was discovered, and the problem of holding up the weight of their voluminous skirts was a constant annoyance for the female population. Fashion was no longer in fashion: basic clothing and not accessories decorated shop windows to attract buyers who lacked either the time or the skill to sew for themselves.

The South's only resources seemed to be cotton and courage.

This was a new Confederacy; Edmund Ruffin's world of the romantic South had collapsed. But the necessity for change was fully appreciated by Jefferson Davis, who reorganized his Cabinet and persuaded Congress to authorize martial law for towns and cities in danger of attack. This was contrary to the traditional attachment of the Old South to civil liberties, individual freedom, and states' rights.

Varina Davis was criticized for hoarding flour—unjustly, since it was for her children. The President was also criticized —by Davis of North Carolina, who became Attorney General. He said: "I do not think I am a very cruel man but I declare that it was the most difficult thing in the world to keep Mr. Davis up to the measure of justice. He wanted to pardon everybody. If ever a wife, a mother, or a sister got into his presence it took but a little while for their tears to wash out the record."

The Tide Turns
1862-1864

In November of 1862 Joseph Johnston, who had recovered, supplanted Bragg as commander of the Army of Tennessee. At the same time General John C. Pemberton took over the Army of the Mississippi. By the spring of 1863 Pemberton and Grant faced each other near Vicksburg. Grant's forces slightly outnumbered Pemberton's, but at Jackson, Mississippi, Johnston had fifteen thousand men at his disposal. When Johnston ordered Pemberton to fall back and join him, the order was disobeyed, but the battle might have gone otherwise had Johnston been a more aggressive commander. Certainly the presence of Robert E. Lee would have changed the odds favorably, but he continued to operate in Virginia.

Mary Chesnut, the famous Southern diarist, tells a story that illustrates Johnston's caution. In his younger days he had come to South Carolina on a hunting expedition. Though reputed to be a very fine shot he brought back no birds, because the conditions never seemed quite right for firing: either the birds were too high or too low, or the dogs were too far or too near so that he refused to risk his reputation as a crack shot. This negative attitude carried over into warfare. Although personally brave and an accomplished general, Johnston was also an egotist, afraid to engage in what might be an unsuccessful battle.

By the end of 1862 the superior numbers of the federal armies had begun to count in battle; besides, the Northern troops had become as efficient as the Southern. Thus the Confederates chose a bad moment to wage an offensive in the North, though in September, 1862, General Jackson captured Harpers Ferry, with its eleven-thousand-man garrison and masses of equipment.

At this time the Southern soldiers did not impress the citizens of the town of Frederick, Maryland. One of them looked with amazement at the ragged army that had routed the Yankees in Virginia. He wrote: "They were the dirtiest men I ever saw, a most ragged, hungry set of wolves. Yet there was a dash about them that the Northern men lacked. They rode like circus riders."

The hopes of Lee's gallant army were dashed by the loss of two sheets of paper. On September 12, two Northern soldiers, a sergeant and a private who had lain down to rest on a recent Confederate campsite near Frederick, spied a long envelope containing three cigars wrapped in two sheets of official-looking paper. With amazement they read Lee's Special Order 191, addressed to Major General D. H. Hill and signed by Colonel C. H. Chilton, Assistant Adjutant General. The order revealed Lee's complex plans for the next four days, the disposition of his forces, and their positions at the hour. The soldiers ran to their colonel, who in turn rushed the document to McClellan.

At Antietam, about fifty miles northwest of Washington, one of the bloodiest battles of the war took place on September 17, 1862. Even though his plan of battle had fallen into McClellan's hands, Lee won a tactical victory. But Antietam proved a severe strategic and political defeat, despite the fact that McClellan's handling of the operation was a model of how not to win a battle. Had the Confederates won decisively at this time, Great Britain would probably have intervened on the side of the South and forced mediation.

Taking advantage of the improved military situation of his armies, Abraham Lincoln issued his Emancipation Proclamation on January 1, 1863, which declared that all slaves, in states still in the areas of rebellion, were "then, thenceforward, and forever, free." The proclamation had a profound effect, not only in the North but in countries abroad.

Meanwhile, in December of 1862, Lee had scored a decisive victory over McClellan's successor, General Ambrose Burnside, at Fredericksburg in Virginia. At one point in the battle Lee saw soldiers from the Carolinas "weep with disappointment when commanded to retire in the face of withering fire." Greatly moved, Lee observed to an aide, "It is well that war is so terrible—we should grow too fond of it."

Once the federals had been forced to retreat at Fredericksburg, Stonewall Jackson urged his commander to allow him to strip his men to the waist despite the zero weather, so that they could be readily distinguished in the dusk from the bluecoats. His object was to launch a final surprise attack on the enemy. Without doubt the result would have been a massacre, but Lee, the humane gentleman-soldier, refused to comply. Grant would not have refused! Even so, Lee did not pass up a great military opportunity, since the federals had already been defeated. He was a supreme tactician, not a commander intent upon annihilating the enemy.

Following his success at Fredericksburg, Lee held on to his strong positions below the Rappahannock. When Burnside's successor Joseph Hooker crossed the river with 130,000 men to attack Lee's bare 60,000, Lee split his force, sending Jack-

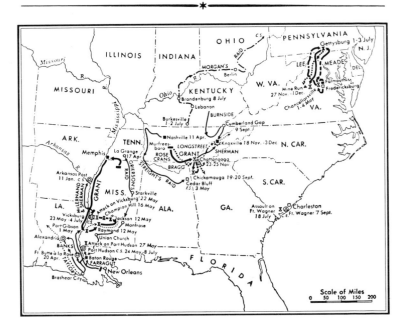

The fighting in 1863

son to hit the Union right while he rolled up the center and
left. The Confederate victory at Chancellorsville (May 2–4,
1863) was complete, but when Stonewall Jackson fell from the
guns of his own men, the Confederacy lost a brilliant general.
After Jackson was shot, the Southern bands played a dirge at
retreat; hearing this, the federal bands played a dirge of their
own in response.

Stonewall Jackson was a phenomenal soldier, yet at the Virginia Military Institute his students had found him dull; he
taught from the book and was called "Tom Fool." He was
indeed a strange man, a silent, awkward fellow, forever suck-
ing a lemon. He looked clumsy, with his mangy forage cap
pulled down, concealing the eyes of a killer. In battle those

eyes gleamed with an intense light—the fire of the burning bush, for Jackson was a warrior out of the Old Testament, and an extremely pious man. At the same time he was brutal; when one of his officers expressed regret at having to kill brave federals, he exclaimed: "No, shoot them all, I do not wish them to be brave."

When news of Chancellorsville reached England, the British concluded that the South would win the war. In a lead editorial the *London Times* advised the North that the Union was "irreparably divided." Many patriotic Northerners abandoned hope that the Confederacy could be conquered.

On May 31, 1863, however, Jefferson Davis wrote Lee about the worsening situation in the West, where Grant was threatening Vicksburg; he suggested that Lee send one of Longstreet's divisions to help in the defense of the city. Lee's reaction was a plan to threaten Washington by achieving another victory like Chancellorsville; with this purpose in mind, he advised Davis to approve his project to invade Pennsylvania. After consulting his Cabinet at several all-day meetings, Davis was doubtful. The President was well aware of the high desertion rate in the Southern army, whose soldiers were worn out from recent fighting, and felt they had done enough by chasing the Yankees out of Virginia. Yet in June, 1863, the Confederate army reached its peak strength of 261,000.

Lee's plan was finally approved and he marched northward. At Gettysburg, Pennsylvania, from July 1 to 3, 1863, the sixth federal commander in the East, George G. Meade, defeated Lee in a crucial conflict. He forced the Confederates, who had lost 29,000 men, to retire to Virginia. Gettysburg was the biggest battle fought up to that time on the North American continent. Following it, Lee wrote to Davis: "I have been prompted by these reflections [on Gettysburg] to propose to Your Excellency the propriety of selecting another commander for the army." Lee felt that this defeat had lost him the confidence of his men; he took the entire blame himself, although some of his subordinates—like Pickett, who led the famous but abortive charge—had made costly mistakes. It was through this quality of selflessness that Lee maintained close relations with his junior officers. Davis replied to Lee: "To ask me to substitute by someone in my judgment more fit to command— is to demand an impossibility."

Lee was talented, modest, tactful, and magnanimous. In fact, he was constantly thinking of others. Had Lee possessed some of Jackson's hardness, he would have been an even greater commander; as it was, he found it difficult to get rid of incompetent officers and to discipline his troops, whom he loved. On the other hand, Lee's concern for his men was returned by their devotion; no commander could so electrify his troops in battle. As Robert Leckie says, in *The Wars of America,* no commander was "more masterful in defense—or more audacious in attack."

Jefferson Davis had consented only reluctantly to the invasion of Pennsylvania. It is curious that Lee favored this maneuver, since he envisioned the war primarily in terms of the Army of Virginia. He had planned no campaign in the West and never even visited the armies there. In the opinion of the Virginia historian Eckenrode, "the one occasion when Lee asserted himself strongly . . . was the one occasion when he happened to be wrong. Davis has been blamed for preferring his own judgment to that of his generals, but in this case when he went against his judgment he made the mistake that decided the outcome of the war."

On the day after Gettysburg the Confederacy suffered a second major disaster: Vicksburg, the fortress on the Mississippi, finally fell to Grant after a long siege. This defeat, suf-

fered by Generals Joseph Johnston and Pemberton, angered
an already bitter South, so that confidence in the President
was badly shaken.

Some months later, in September of 1863, Bragg for once
attacked vigorously at Chickamauga in Tennessee; he drove
the federals back, and captured the city of Chattanooga. Davis
called this "one of the most brilliant and decisive victories of
the war," and appointed his friend Bragg chief of staff at
Richmond. Upon hearing of this Varina, who rarely offered
her husband advice on military matters, protested, feeling that
in such a high army post Bragg would create disunity. Generally, Jefferson Davis heeded Varina's opinions, particularly
on political matters. This time he did not and was right, for
Bragg was a good organizer and proved highly efficient as
chief of staff.

Davis erred in ignoring the political astuteness of his people. He had always felt that his right to rule derived from his
official position. His years at West Point had engendered an
aristocratic attitude, rather than the pliancy needed by a poli-
tician. Yet on the whole he had been an effective President,
and while he lost the confidence of his people toward the end
of the war, he did gain their affection.

Of Jefferson Davis, John Garraty observed that "he quar-
reled frequently with his subordinates, held grudges, and
allowed his personal feelings to influence his judgment, often
to the detriment of the Southern cause." True, Davis was
often querulous with his subordinates, particularly with Joseph
Johnston. But he had always respected Johnston as a soldier,
and in November, 1863, placed him in command of a new
theater of war—the Confederate heartland between the Ap-
palachians and the Mississippi.

———————

By late 1863 transportation in the South had broken down and food prices, with butter costing $20 a pound, had become astronomical. Nevertheless, morale stayed high; blacks for the most part remained loyal, and Lee reported that nearly all his men had re-enlisted. Dinner parties, with champagne at $350 a case, flourished in Richmond, and it was said that the city had never been so gay. No one was thinking, no one would have accepted the fact, that the day was not far off when the Confederacy would fall, marking the triumph of businessman over planter.

Under the surface, however, disaffection and defeatism grew. Governor Vance of North Carolina suggested that peace negotiations be initiated despite the strength and excellent equipment of the Southern armies, whose main problem was rations. Actually it was the North, despondent over the loss of Chattanooga and war weary, which came closer to yielding now—surprising, since it seemed more and more probable that the Union forces would eventually emerge victorious. Within a few months the Northern urge to make peace became insistent.

Rumor now spread that the war would end shortly, and many Southerners started to plant cotton and tobacco on a large scale, preparing for reopened world markets. Jefferson Davis was alarmed because he knew such crops would diminish food supplies. Expecting the war to go on several more years, he addressed the people, urging them to continue producing mainly food.

The food crisis became more acute. Finally a group of Richmond women, wives of workers at the Tredegar Ironworks, got together in April of 1863. Alarmed by the price and scarcity of bread, several hundred of them marched to Governor John Letcher's mansion on Capitol Square to air their complaints. The governor listened sympathetically, but could do nothing. During the demonstration a Richmond lady asked a girl on the fringe of the crowd, "Is there some kind of celebration?" "There is," replied the girl. "We celebrate the right to live. We are starving. As soon as enough of us get together we are going to the bakeries and each of us will take a loaf of bread."

One of the rioters stepped forward. It was Mary Jackson, a tall, daring woman who, accompanied by the others, marched on to the commercial district. Armed with knives, hatchets, and pistols, they broke into shops, taking what they pleased; most of them wanted only food, but some seized jewelry and clothing. The petition had become a riot.

Letcher hurried to the commercial district and without success attempted to placate the women. The mob continued to the city's marketplaces, where a company of reserve troops attempted to disband them; the rioters retaliated by pushing a wagon across the street as a barricade. At that tense moment Jefferson Davis appeared. Climbing on top of the wagon, he tried to calm the crowd, but could not be heard above the din. At last, in order to attract attention, Davis emptied his pockets and threw money to the mob. He then pulled out his watch and, looking back at the soldiers behind him, cried out: "We do not desire to injure anyone, but this lawlessness must stop. I will give you five minutes to disperse, otherwise you will be fired upon." No one moved and the captain in command ordered, "Load." After the first endless minute, the crowd broke up. The bread riot was over, due to Davis's quick, courageous action.

Confederate women had climbed down from their romantic pedestals and had begun to make themselves felt as a force. "In the Old South," as Emory Thomas writes in *The Confederacy,* "the best expression of Southern romanticism was the planter's veneration for his woman. Believing, or wanting to believe himself a latter day feudal lord and neo-cavalier, he required his woman to be a lily maid and object of his courtly love [—and nothing else.]"

News of the riot spread; that spring similar ones broke out in Atlanta, Macon, Columbus, Augusta, and other Southern cities. It is notable that these disturbances took place at a time when the Confederacy had achieved self-sufficiency in military production, and when its industrial capacity was approaching full stride. Credit for this progress belongs to the handful of men in the government who finally managed to get everything but the broken-down railroads working again.

Nevertheless, at the end of 1863 the Confederacy was facing bankruptcy: Confederate notes had depreciated by 98.4 percent, as against Federal notes' depreciation of 61 percent. After the outbreak of war, the South should have sent abroad as much cotton as possible, to be held as collateral for its future financial requirements. But by 1864 the Northern blockade made cotton exports impossible. Partly because of this, Jefferson Davis was obliged to call an emergency session of Congress in February. He reported desertions, disloyalty, and discontent, and warned that the government was in danger of dissolution. He requested the suspension of *habeas corpus* in disaffected areas—the equivalent of placing the country under a dictatorship. Alarmed, Congress voted to grant the President additional powers, but these proved insufficient to deal with the crisis.

For some weeks Davis had been watching General Joseph Johnston's operations with growing doubt. At last he asked Johnston, "Will you surrender Atlanta without a fight?" Upon receiving an evasive reply, Davis consulted Lee and members of his Cabinet as to the advisability of removing Johnston and appointing General John B. Hood to replace him. All were in favor. Named to the command, Hood followed his orders, waging a series of hotly contested battles in defense of Atlanta. Only thirty-three years old, he tended to be reckless, but military experts assessed Hood's fight for Atlanta as "sound— even brilliant."

Davis's decision to replace Johnston was deeply resented. No single action by the President was more sharply attacked; when Johnston was relieved of this command, his men wept. Grant observed: "When I heard the [Confederate] government had removed Johnston I was as happy as if I had reinforced Sherman with a large army corps. . . . Joe Johnston gave me more anxiety than any of the others. I was never half so anxious about Lee." Later Grant wrote in his memoirs: "My own judgment is that Johnston acted very wisely; he husbanded his men and saved as much of his territory as he could, without fighting decisive battles in which all might be lost. . . . Hood was unquestionably a brave, gallant soldier, and not destitute of ability, but unfortunately, his policy was to fight the enemy wherever he saw him, without thinking much of the consequences of defeat."

Grant proved right. On August 31, 1864, Hood was forced to abandon Atlanta after losing 8,000 men in his fight to hold the city.

During the summer of 1864, Judah P. Benjamin, then Secretary of State, proposed that the slaves be liberated, hoping this move would finally bring foreign recognition. Soon after, the question of arming the slaves was agitated. Supported by Lee, Davis favored liberation, although he realized that this would mean the end of the Southern way of life. But there was no alternative. By now 100,000 Confederate soldiers —one enlistee out of nine—had deserted (compared with one out of seven in the North): a practice much encouraged on both sides by the provision for avoiding military service

Library of Congress

*Union General
Ulysses S. Grant*

through paying a few hundred dollars. As the Confederacy continued to weaken against a foe who could replace his losses and add new reinforcements from his pool of immigrant soldiers, or from the 100,000 black soldiers recruited, drastic action became imperative.

It is surprising that no mass slave revolts had occurred during the war. When Lincoln issued his Emancipation Proclamation, a Philadelphia paper reported that "the Negroes showed a strange aversion to freedom." Throughout the conflict the black population in the South had remained docile, and for the most part loyal to the Confederacy, although they flocked to their liberators when the victorious Union army appeared.

In 1864 Davis asked Congress to purchase 40,000 slaves

for noncombatant military service, with liberation as a reward upon their discharge. In making his request, he said: "Until our white population shall prove insufficient for the armies, to employ the Negro as a soldier . . . would scarcely seem wise or advantageous." The resulting debate in Congress lasted almost as long as the Confederacy. In the words of Emory Thomas, Jefferson Davis had "made a tentative beginning at becoming the great emancipator for the southern Blacks."

The winter of 1864–65 was desperate for the South. The Union had a splendidly equipped army, whereas Davis had lost control of Congress, so that any measure favored by him was doomed. On February 6, 1865, a bill to arm the slaves was introduced into Congress by the Administration. In a letter to a congressman, Lee requested black troops, maintaining that

The fighting in 1864–1865

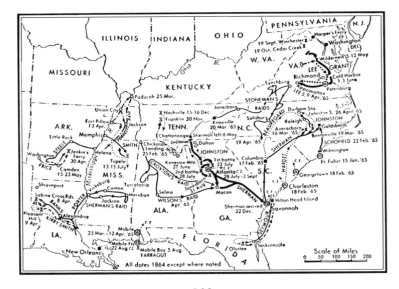

they would make efficient soldiers, and expressed the opinion that they should be allowed to fight as free men and not as slaves. Five weeks later Congress agreed to arm the slaves, but not to emancipate them. (By 1864 there were 200,000 blacks in the Union armies.)

It was Jefferson Davis and his War Office who closed the debate: General Order No. 12 implemented the decision that the slaves were to serve in the armed forces as free men. The order was issued on February 23; two days later, the first Negro company was formed—shortly before Richmond ceased to be the capital of the Confederacy. In contrast to this order, not long before issuing his Emancipation Proclamation, Lincoln had maintained that "the liberation of the slaves is the destruction of property—property acquired by descent or by purchase, the same as any other property." Indeed, Lincoln's opinions differed widely from those of the Abolitionists, and his Emancipation Proclamation was primarily designed to provide a rallying cry for the Northern war effort.

Davis's decision, as expressed in General Order No. 12, was evidence of his adaptability, his ability to change his mind when change was called for.

Defeat and
Imprisonment
1864-1867

When the Civil War started, Confederate General Richard Ewell observed: "There is one West Pointer, I think in Missouri, little known, and whom I hope the Northern people will not find out. I mean Sam Grant. I knew him well at the Academy and in Mexico. I should fear him more than any of their officers I have yet heard of. He is not a man of genius, but he is clear-headed, quick and daring."

According to historian Robert Leckie, "The Union very nearly did not 'find out' about Sam Grant. Bored by the peacetime garrison life ... Grant had begun to drink and been forced out of the Army rather than face a court-martial for drunkenness. . . . He drifted toward the brink of despair as a despised clerk in the family harness shop in Galena, Illinois."

At the time when Grant was drinking so heavily that he was about to be expelled from the army, Davis, as Secretary of War, had arranged for him to resign instead. No one had thought much of Grant in those days, except when a crisis arose; he was one of those men who would unfailingly rise to an emergency. In this respect, Grant was in sharp contrast to the self-confident McClellan. After Sumter, Grant had told a friend: "To tell you the truth, I would rather like a regiment, yet there are few men really competent to command a thousand men, and I doubt whether I am one of them." Nevertheless, Governor Yates of Illinois had taken a chance and made Grant, at thirty-nine, a colonel of volunteers.

The colonel's regiment had its doubts when Ulysses S. Grant showed up in camp in an old, worn-out civilian coat and a ragged hat. "What a colonel!" the men howled. But when they observed their colonel's firm, hard mouth and calm glance, and heard the clarity of his voice and sharp orders, they realized that this was a man to be reckoned with.

At the end of 1863, when Ulysses S. Grant had been appointed commander-in-chief of the Northern armies, he entrusted the Southwest to Sherman and Thomas.

In May, 1864, Grant crossed the Rapidan River about forty miles north of Richmond, and marched confidently into the tangled Wilderness, planning to clear it and attack Lee on open ground. But the wily Lee defeated the federals at Spottsylvania, after a five-day struggle which marked one of the first uses of trenches in warfare. Despite the almost total destruction of two of his corps, Grant kept moving forward with bulldog persistence.

Grant's casualties in the Wilderness alone came to 60,000. He had good reason to despair, since to date he had achieved no more than McClellan had in 1862, while McClellan's losses had been slight by comparison. Because of this bloodshed, Grant was named "Butcher Grant"—unfairly, because he had no choice in this situation but to crush Lee. Lee's strategy had been brilliant, but Grant's mystifying tactics from Spottsylvania to Cold Harbor were equally so. The Wilderness Campaign was long and savage, and in the course of it Grant, whose army was numerically far superior, lost more men than the total of Lee's whole force. Yet in spite of the grim toll,

Grant had the right idea: to pin Lee down and compel him to fight the kind of war he could not win.

By June, 1864, Grant faced the Confederates at Petersburg, twenty miles south of Richmond, his object being to approach the capital from the rear and cut its links with the rest of the South. In the initial attack on Petersburg, Grant again suffered heavy losses, after which he was forced to dig in for what proved to be a nine-month siege—the longest of the war.

The fortunes of the Confederacy were now at a very low ebb: Lee had his back to the wall. In this situation, recriminations between the civilian and military branches of the government might have been expected. Instead, the spirit of good will and cooperation that had always existed between Davis and Lee was stronger than ever. Yet at no time during the conflict had Lee predicted victory for the South: from 1864 on, his correspondence, though not pessimistic, anticipated the final outcome. After all, he had lived in the North and was familiar with its vast resources.

At this dark and critical moment Alexander Stephens castigated the President in a three-hour speech. He said that he regarded each state as a nation. Previously he had declared: "A citizen of the state has no allegiance to the Confederate States government ... and can owe no military service to it except as required by his own state." Now he added: "Tell me not to put confidence in the President. ... The most illtimed, delusive and dangerous words that can be uttered are, 'Can you not trust the President?' "

In the summer of 1864, feeling in the North ran strong for making peace. Lincoln feared that in the November elections General McClellan, the Democratic candidate, would be elected President. McClellan stood on a platform which, under influence of the Copperheads—Northerners sympathetic to the

South—favored ending the war on any terms, and making peace "on the basis of the Federal Union of the States." Mc-Clellan himself repudiated the peace plank, but sought to capitalize on Northern defeatism. He did in fact come close to winning the Presidency: Lincoln's popular majority was 400,000 out of 4 million votes.

Dissatisfaction over the course of the war had reached the point where Grant's position as commander-in-chief was in jeopardy. But he was now pressing the Confederates hard, and no longer shared the general view of Lee's ability as a commander. He later observed: "Lee was of a slow, cautious nature, without imagination or humor, always the same, with grave dignity. I never could see in his achievements what justifies his reputation."

In 1864 the Northern high command decided to wage total war. Accordingly, General Philip Sheridan was ordered to the Shenandoah Valley. Late that year he put this granary of the South to the torch and left it a scene of blackened desolation. Even more fatal for the Confederacy was Grant's order to Sherman to devastate the land from Chattanooga to the sea, and so destroy the productive capacity and morale of the South. Sherman obeyed, but saw no glory in war. "It is all hell," he said. One of the cities overrun by Sherman's army was Columbia, South Carolina. The burning and looting of Columbia outraged its citizens, but did not convince them of the futility of their cause. "We mean to destroy all your food," said a Northern soldier to a young Carolinian who had dared confront him after her hometown had been pillaged. "Very well," she replied, "we will live on acorns."

William Tecumseh Sherman was the most original of Civil War generals: he saw that industrialized war had shifted the

*Union General
William Tecumseh
Sherman*

Library of Congress

Culver Pictures, Inc.

*Union General
Philip H. Sheridan*

main objective to destroying the enemy's economy. In Georgia he bypassed his foe but attacked his industrial potential and population. This was *blitzkrieg*.

With the fall of Atlanta on September 1, 1864, agitation in the South to make Lee military dictator rose to a clamor. The general quelled this by promptly declining to serve in such capacity. When Lee was then asked whether Jefferson Davis had been a good President, he replied: "I know of no man who could have done better."

During these last months of the war, in 1865, a deeply worried Davis sent a secret emissary to Europe, promising to the Europeans the abolition of slavery in exchange for recognition. Soon after, early in 1865, Lincoln dispatched Francis P. Blair to Richmond in order to sound out the Confederacy. A few weeks later Davis sent a three-man mission to the North, consisting of John Campbell, Alexander Stephens, and R. M. T. Hunter. The meeting was held on the steamboat *River Queen* in Hampton Roads, where the three Confederate commissioners were joined in the saloon by Lincoln and Seward. Stephens asked: "Is there no way of putting an end to the present trouble, and bringing about a restoration of general good feeling and harmony?" Lincoln replied: "There is but one way— for those who are resisting the laws of the Union to cease that resistance." He offered $400 million compensation for the freed slaves, but emphasized: "The restoration of the Union is a *sine qua non* with me."

With these words the peace conference was doomed.

It had all turned out as Jefferson Davis had expected; the only recourse left was to fight on. Davis took the occasion to make an appeal to the people of Richmond—a stirring speech which Edward Pollard, an editor of the *Richmond Examiner* and a Davis antagonist, praised highly. Vice-President Stephens, Davis's archenemy, wrote of the speech: "It was not only bold and undaunted in tone, but had that loftiness of sentiment and rare form of expression, as well as magnetic influence of delivery, by which the people are moved to their profoundest depths." During the last year of the war, Jefferson Davis's speeches were in fact inspiring, for he had abandoned the aloofness that had kept him from opening his heart to the people.

That spring of 1865 Davis was in poor health. Nevertheless, he kept up his exhausting schedule and seemed in surprisingly good spirits. This was remarkable, because the final days of the Confederate Congress were taken up with recriminations between that body and the President. Furthermore, Davis received a tragic blow when his little son Joseph fell off a porch of their Richmond house and was killed. Varina gave way to uncontrolled grief, but according to Burton Harrison, secretary to the President, "the terrible self-control of Jefferson Davis was even more heartbreaking."

Davis might have been a more popular political figure, had he not kept such a tight rein on himself. But the question is probably academic, for he had learned long ago that he had to curb his emotions and his hot temper. The episode at Fort Crawford, when young Lieutenant Davis's attentions to the pretty Indian squaw had infuriated her brother, and his frequent outbreaks later against fellow senators, had proved to Jefferson Davis the necessity of achieving absolute self-control.

In spite of the desperate plight of the Confederacy in 1865, Richmond was still putting up a gallant front. Its streets were crowded with soldiers in uniform, with gaily dressed officers and beautiful women turned out elegantly, if not in the latest fashions. However, by the end of March Davis was forced to send Varina and the children to Charlotte, North Carolina; he gave her all his money except for a five-dollar gold piece. He also handed her a pistol and showed her how to load, aim, and fire it, telling her, "You can at least, if reduced to the last extremity, force your assailants to kill you."

On Sunday, April 2, 1865, Jefferson Davis, who was attending church services, received a message from Lee that Grant had broken through his lines at Five Forks, and that Richmond must be abandoned. Lee's forces were down to 30,000 men, starving and in rags, yet not far away warehouses were bulging with supplies—a painfully ironic situation, accented by the nearness of Grant and his huge army.

The President rose from his pew and with quickened step left the church. That afternoon he told his Cabinet that the government must move immediately to Danville, Virginia. Later that day, as the Davis train crawled along the Danville railroad at ten miles an hour, Sheridan's cavalry were scouring the countryside, looking for the President and his Cabinet. When he finally reached Danville, Davis' hastily set up his executive offices and issued his last proclamation, announcing that the South had now entered upon a new phase of the struggle. He added that the army, relieved of the necessity of guarding cities and other strategic areas, would move from point to point and "strike—in detail—detachments and garrisons of the enemy." To reassure the people, Davis added: "Nothing is now needed to render our triumph certain but the exhibition of our unquenchable resolve." But few believed him. The Confederacy was now reduced to waging guerrilla warfare.

Forty-eight hours before Jefferson Davis's proclamation, federal troops had marched into Richmond. Half the city was on fire, and many of the people had turned into wild, half-starved creatures and had started to loot. Drunken men shot off their muskets as they reeled through the burning buildings.

The burning of Richmond, 1865

The city was placed under martial law and patrolled by black Union troops, while the white inhabitants stayed in their homes, watching the soldiers pass. Every window was filled with heads, but it was a silent crowd. There was something oppressive about these thousands of watchers making no sound, either of welcome or hatred.

In the midst of the chaos hardly anyone noticed "a tall, bony man wearing a long black cape and a stovepipe hat, followed by a squad of marines. He walked along East Clay Street, passing buildings blackened by fire. The few Richmond citizens who did recognize the man let him pass unmolested, having accepted defeat without resentment. From Clay Street this man went on to Jefferson Davis's house and wandered through its rooms with childlike curiosity."

After completing his inspection of the city, Abraham Lincoln—who, according to a witness on the scene, seemed pale and utterly worn out—visited Grant's headquarters to discuss the conditions of surrender to be offered to Lee. The terms he directed were generous, and Lincoln intimated that Davis should be persuaded to leave the country, suggesting that a federal boat be provided him for this purpose. Lincoln wanted Davis to escape, "unbeknownst to me," he said.

Meanwhile, since leaving the capital, the Confederate President had become unaccountably calm, appearing even optimistic at this low ebb of his fortunes. One evening Davis's hostess at a dinner asked, "Mr. Davis, would Lee's surrender end the war?" "By no means," he replied. "We'll fight it out on the Mississippi River." He had never lost faith in his cause.

Jefferson Davis had certain shortcomings as a military leader. His absorption in military details had drained his energy and diverted his mind from more important concerns. In addition, he had interfered with the War Department, although not with the decisions of his other Cabinet officers. On the other hand, as commander-in-chief he had acted decisively in crises, carrying out his decisions with strong will. In the critical hours of the Confederacy, Davis would consult the best minds available, and the plan that was adopted usually succeeded. Finally, though he made suggestions to his generals, he did not interfere with their plans of battle.

Under the strain of war—at least until near the end—President Davis changed noticeably. He developed a closed, sphinxlike personality, becoming, in the words of Clement Eaton, a recent biographer of Davis, "a furnace of emotions inside, an enigma to historians."

————————

On April 3, 1865, Lee's ragged veterans reached Amelia Courthouse, twenty-one miles west of Petersburg. There was not a single ration for Lee's ravenously hungry men. Two days later the forage wagons arrived, but they were nearly empty.

In early April, Grant asked Lee to help him in stopping "any further effusion of blood" by surrendering. Lee agreed to discuss the matter, but secretly determined to fight on by adopting guerrilla tactics. Only recently he had told Davis: "With my army in the mountains of Virginia I could carry on this war for twenty years longer." But, as the President later explained: "When Lee found the line which obstructed his retreat could not be broken, he said there was nothing to do but surrender."

This finally happened at Appomattox, some seventy miles west of Petersburg. Lee and his army were surrounded, and on April 9, 1865, the Confederate general and his staff agreed to meet with Grant and his staff in a neighboring farmhouse. Grant had started out for this meeting "quite jubilant," but in the presence of his antagonist, who had fought so bravely, his mood changed to sadness. This mood was shared by his men, and Colonel Robert Bingham, an aide to Lee, watched as the Confederates stacked their arms for the last time. He said, later: "I saw tears of sympathy and pity streaming from the eyes of the federal soldiers who stood in line on each side of us. They had pursued us and overwhelmed us, but they were touched with the feeling of our infirmity, and the victorious Americans mingled their tears with the tears of the vanquished Americans."

Grant and Lee started their conversation by reminiscing about the old army days. It seemed at one point as though Grant had almost forgotten the business at hand, so that Lee was finally obliged to ask about the terms of surrender. They were generous: the Confederate officers were to keep their side arms, and the soldiers their horses; ample food supplies were to be distributed to the starving Southerners. Lee particularly appreciated the fact that his soldiers could keep their horses. "This would have the best possible effect on the men," he said, "it will do much toward conciliating our people." General Lee then looked at his "Farewell to the Army," prepared by an aide. "Strike out those harsher expressions," he ordered, "there must be no more bitterness between North and South. We are now one country."

Their business concluded, Lee rode away on his great horse Traveler, as thousands of Union soldiers presented arms.

Robert E. Lee with his horse Traveler

When Jefferson Davis heard about Lee's surrender he wept, but refused to admit defeat. Nor would the Southern die-hard Edmund Ruffin surrender. When he realized that the "cause" was lost forever, he closed his diary on June 17, 1865, declaring unmitigated hatred of Yankee rule. "Then Ruffin sat straight in his chair," according to Emory Thomas, "placed the muzzle of his silver mounted gun in his mouth. With a forked stick he pulled the trigger and joined the Confederacy in violent death."

It was mid-April now. Davis decided to confer with General Joseph Johnston at Greensboro, North Carolina. He had not heard that Johnston had requested Sherman to grant a temporary suspension of hostilities, nor that Sherman had willingly consented. When he arrived, after a few words of greeting Davis said to Johnston: "I have requested you and General Beauregard ... to join me this evening, that we might have the benefit of your views on the situation in this country." Johnston replied sharply: "My views are, sir, that our people are tired of the war, feel themselves whipped, and will not fight. ... My men are daily deserting in large numbers ... since Lee's surrender, they regard the war as at an end."

Three days later the news reached Davis that Johnston and Sherman had signed an agreement; Sherman had consented to general pacification. In a letter to Varina dated April 23, Davis wrote: "[The terms] are secret and may be rejected by the Yankee government. To us they are hard enough, though freed from wanton humiliation, and expressly recognizing the state governments, and the rights of person and property as secured by the Constitutions of the United States and the several states."

In his memorandum of April 22, 1865, concerning the Johnston-Sherman agreement, Judah P. Benjamin declared that Sherman's terms were "the best and most favorable that we could hope to obtain by a continuance of the struggle." He added that, while Davis was "powerless to act in making peace on any other basis than that of independence," he could, as commander-in-chief, "ratify the military convention . . . and execute its provisions. He can end hostilities."

Warning the President that the army under Johnston's command was down from 70,000 to 20,000, Benjamin concluded by saying: "We could not at the present moment gather together an army of 30,000 by concentrating all our forces east of the Mississippi. . . . We have lost possession in Virginia and North Carolina of our chief resources for the supply of powder and lead. We can obtain no aid from the Trans-Mississippi Department, from which we are cut off by the fleets of gunboats that patrol the river. We have not a supply of arms sufficient for putting into the field even 10,000 additional men."

The memo ended on a grim note: "The President should by proclamation inform the states and the people of the Confederacy of the facts above recited; should ratify the convention so far as he has authority to act as commander-in-chief, and should declare his inability with the means remaining at his disposal to defend the Confederacy or maintain its independence, and should resign."

Soon after delivering his message, Benjamin quit his post in the Cabinet, and having taken leave of the President, started for the coast, where he boarded a boat bound for England. In the years to come he practiced law there and carved out for himself a brilliant career; no other alien ever achieved such success at the English bar.

Jefferson Davis received messages from various members of his Cabinet supporting Benjamin's views. Secretary of War Breckinridge wrote: "Our ports are closed, and all the sources of foreign supply lost to us. The enemy occupy all, or the greater part of Missouri, Kentucky, Tennessee, Virginia, and North Carolina, and move almost at will through the other states, to the east of the Mississippi. . . . I do not think it would be possible to assemble, equip and maintain an army of 30,000 men at any point east of the Mississippi River."

Under pressure, Davis accepted the terms of the Johnston-Sherman agreement. As he understood it, the agreement meant that the States of the Confederacy would re-enter the Union "upon the same footing on which they stood before seceding from it." Davis affixed his signature. But barely an hour before the document had reached Johnston's headquarters, the general had learned from a disappointed Sherman that the federal government had categorically rejected this peace proposal.

Sherman then stated that he was bound to resume hostilities unless Johnston surrendered on the same terms as had Lee to Grant. Johnston wired Davis for instructions, and was ordered by him to withdraw immediately. But despite the President's order, on April 26 Johnston decided to surrender. Even after learning about these events, Davis did not abandon all hope. He planned "to maintain his ground with small forces after the manner of Washington in the Revolution, and wring eventual recognition from the North." Fine words, but impossible.

It had been a terrible war. The combined Union and Confederate casualties amounted to 33 to 40 percent of the forces involved. The Northerners had lost 359,000 dead; the Southerners, 258,000. Not only were the casualties shocking; the treatment of war prisoners by both sides had been deplorable. At Andersonville Prison, a twenty-acre plot in the backwoods of Georgia which housed 30,000 federal prisoners, the death rate rose from 300 a month to 3,000 between March and August, 1864, while in Camp Douglas, Illinois, during the

Andersonville Prison

in Georgia

harvest season of the same year, 1,000 of the 5,000 Confederates imprisoned there suffered severely from scurvy. More than 26,000 Southerners died in Northern prisons, and while both North and South proposed prisoner exchanges, the negotiations came to nothing. Grant was opposed to any compromise on the grounds that every Confederate prisoner released on parole would become an active soldier again. "If we commence a series of exchanges," he wrote in 1864, "we will have to fight until the whole South is exterminated."

After the surrenders of Johnston and Lee, the President and his party wandered from town to town. On April 19 in Virginia he learned of Lincoln's assassination and was moved to comment: "I certainly have no regard for Mr. Lincoln but there are a great many men whose end I would much rather have heard than his. I fear it will be disastrous to our people, and I regret it deeply." For Davis, Lincoln's death was the last crowning calamity of a despairing and defeated cause.

Davis had mellowed. Perhaps, in referring to Lincoln in kindly terms, he was only contrasting him with Andrew Johnson, who on assuming power had proclaimed Jefferson Davis an outlaw and accused him of being involved in Lincoln's murder. Johnson offered a big reward for Davis's capture: "$100,000 Reward in Gold," the proclamation read, "will be paid to any person or persons who will apprehend and deliver Jefferson Davis to any of the military authorities of the United States." Moreover, the new President had told a Washington street crowd that he would hang Jefferson Davis and all the "diabolical" crew at Richmond, if he ever got the chance.

Davis later confirmed the story that a Colonel Alston had written to him, offering to assassinate Lincoln. In reply Davis had forwarded the letter to the Confederate War Office, with orders that Alston be arrested and court-martialed. Remembering this, it did not occur to him that he could ever be suspected of the murder of Lincoln. But many Northerners, not knowing the details of the assassination, were spreading the word that it was a further example of Southern barbarism. For them it was one more reason why Jefferson Davis should be captured and hanged.

A "wanted" man now, Jefferson Davis thought first of his family, from whom he had become separated in the chaos. Despairingly, he made his way to Charlotte. As he journeyed through North Carolina the President received a cool welcome; in Greensboro all doors were closed to him and his government, for fear of federal vengeance had made the inhabitants wary. Davis was exhausted by his disappointments and by anxiety for his family. Finally a member of his staff succeeded in finding a bed for him in a small house. Although terribly tired—he had taken no vacation during the war—he appeared cheerful, and observed: "I cannot feel like a beat man."

The federal cavalry was now in hot pursuit, but Davis did not hurry. At Irwinville, Georgia, he finally caught up with Varina. And there, on May 10, 1865, he and his party were surprised at early dawn by a detachment of cavalry. Davis dressed hurriedly in the dark, putting on his wife's raincoat; at the same time she threw a shawl over his head. (According to the Northern press, the terrified Davis tried to escape by disguising himself in women's clothes.) Then, while the soldiers were rudely questioning Varina, he slipped away, heading for the woods. He almost made it, but one of the federals spotted him and shouted, "Halt!" as he raised his gun. Varina shrieked and Davis rebuked the soldiers for having first insulted and then frightened his wife.

Davis still had not given up. He drew his bowie knife and

attempted to cut his way out of the ambush. But he was up against a heavily armed unit, and his knife was no match for their revolvers. As he prepared to attack the horseman next to him, in order to steal his horse and escape, Varina pinioned his arms. For Jefferson Davis, the war had at last come to an end.

After his capture Davis became very unpopular in the Confederacy; he was called a despot. But his cruel treatment as a prisoner by the U.S. government made him a martyr after a time and restored him to immense popularity in the South.

The Union officers who had captured Davis took him to Macon, Georgia, and turned him over to the commanding officer of the region. From there he was moved to Augusta, where the captive Stephens joined him. After another move, to Norfolk, it was finally decided to transfer him to Fortress Monroe, Virginia. Here he was to be imprisoned for two years, confined in a casement cell with one small barred window looking out on a moat, while two roughshod guards tramped ceaselessly within. General Nelson A. Miles ordered irons riveted around the prisoner's ankles, but when the blacksmith approached him, Davis fell upon the man and guards had to be called in. Gasping for breath and clutching his throat, the ex-President cried out, "Oh, God! Let me die! Shoot me!"

Fortress Monroe was built like a medieval castle. Davis was allowed no books except the Bible, no visitors, and no food from outside. Yet in his letters Davis showed that he had become resigned to his fate—unlike Varina, who suffered from a frantic sense of injustice. He found consolation in the Christian faith—and in smoking his meerschaum pipe. In the end, he came to possess a kind of mystic spirituality. In fact, Davis's triumph during his last twenty-five years was a spiritual one.

For five days he remained chained, and was not allowed a

*Cartoon of Jefferson Davis trying to avoid
capture by Union troops*

knife and fork for fear he would cut his throat. The press was full of stories, with lurid details of the shackling, and the government was censured for this insult to the ex-President of the Confederacy and to the South. Finally, on May 28, 1865, Secretary of War Stanton ordered the chains removed. Nevertheless, the Northern press continued its attacks on Davis. Even two months after his capture, the *New York Times* wrote: "We had looked for a growl of thunder from the London *Times* and lambent lightning from the *Saturday Review*. . . . He committed treason, he rules the disloyal States with a despot's rod of iron." Davis's damp, badly ventilated cell was brightly lit night and day so that sleep was almost impossible. Only after months of pleading by Horace Greeley and other enlightened Northerners, was he placed in somewhat better quarters.

As the days passed, Dr. Craven, who was attending Davis, looked forward to visits with him. Craven wrote in his journal that he was enchanted by the former President's conversation and amazed by his extraordinary memory. He marveled at Davis's range of knowledge, "from warfare to optics—to the culture of oysters, to Hogarth, to engineering." And he was touched by the ex-President's reply to his question of why he collected bread crumbs in his cell: he was keeping them to feed a mouse he had domesticated.

Dr. Craven grew increasingly anxious about Davis's health, and told Varina her husband was steadily failing. "The only thing left," he said, "is to give him mental and bodily rest, and exercise at will." On November 7, 1865, Varina wrote to Jefferson: "My dear Husband, Husband, dear Saintly Husband, if I were to give reins to my pen, surged on by my quivering, longing heart, what might the indifferent eyes which first peruse these whilom sacred confidences, see to. Well, well, I do not use the terms of bygone times, but the heart which dictated them is the same which has throbbed for you alone since it could feel a woman's love."

A touching, remarkable letter, written twenty years after her marriage.

Andrew Johnson now tried to get the ex-President to apply for pardon but Davis refused, since for him to do so would have meant confession of prior guilt. Johnson still claimed to possess facts implicating Davis in Lincoln's murder, but knew he had no such evidence and realized how absurd his charge would look if brought to court.

Early in 1866 Varina was allowed to visit her children in Canada. After her return she started a campaign to release her husband from prison. By spring Washington opinion had changed and Varina was allowed to visit Jefferson. She had done everything possible to obtain more humane treatment for him, and had even pleaded his cause with President Johnson.

Horace Greeley, the powerful New York journalist, wrote a strong editorial urging Davis's immediate release, and Charles O'Connor, an able lawyer also from New York, volunteered his services. The efforts of these people on behalf of the ex-President succeeded. Davis was released from prison and shortly thereafter, on May 21, 1867, was brought before the federal court at Richmond and released on bail. The bail of $100,000 for his appearance at a formal trial was signed by Greeley and Gerrit Smith, both of whom had been prominent Abolitionists. The trial never took place.

In her memoir Varina Davis tells how many years after the war, in 1890, she received a letter from a Mr. H. Clarke, a friend of Jefferson Davis, saying, "I came out of Richmond with him . . . and I was close to his person, until he parted with me on May 6, 1865, near Sandersville, Georgia. . . . On that retreat (if so leisurely a retirement could be so called), I saw an organized government deteriorate and fall to pieces little by little, until there was left only a single member of the Cabinet, his private secretary and a few members of his staff. Calm, self-poised—advising and consoling—he appeared incomparably grander . . . than when he reviewed victorious armies."

Aftermath
1867-1889

In Richmond, Jefferson Davis was welcomed at the Spottswood Hotel by a bigger crowd than that which had greeted him as their new President five years before.

Davis was free now, but a man without a country, for Andrew Johnson's pardon of 1865 denied the rights of citizenship to many who had supported the Southern cause. Neither Davis nor Lee regained his citizenship in his own lifetime; in fact, more than a hundred years passed before the American government finally voted to restore their civil rights—to Lee in 1976, and to Davis in 1977. They deserved this overdue recognition, for after the war both had sincerely tried to persuade the South to accept defeat and support the new Union.

From Richmond the Davises went to Canada, where they were lent a house in Montreal, thanks to some Southern friends. They did not stay long, however, because the winter there proved too harsh for the enfeebled Davis. The family then moved to Cuba, and from there to New Orleans. Here the ex-President was greeted as a hero, as he had been upon returning from the Mexican War many years before.

His visit to Brierfield was tragic: the place was overgrown with weeds and brambles, and the houses had been burned down. His doctor now advised a year of rest and travel in Europe, so the family packed up once more and boarded a steamer for England. Arriving in London in 1869, Davis was warmly welcomed by Parliament. He enjoyed England, where he was entertained by many peers, including the Earl of Shrewsbury, the Duke of Northumberland, the Marquess of Westminster, and the Duke of Sutherland. In Paris he was invited to the imperial court, and a military parade was held in his honor. But the ex-President declined to meet the Emperor, who had been unwilling to recognize the Confederacy, although he had permitted French shipyards to build ships for the Confederates—a very important concession.

When they returned to the United States, the Davises settled in Memphis, where a fine house had been purchased for them by the people of the city. This Davis felt he could not accept. But he did become head of a local insurance company, having declined the presidency of the University of Sewanee because it paid only $2,000 per annum—not enough, given his pressing need for money.

The year 1874 was a disastrous one for Davis: the insurance company failed and his brother Joseph died. The final blow came when his son, William Howell, expired a few days after contracting diphtheria, leaving only Winnie of his seven children. A saddened man, Davis returned to Brierfield and tried to earn a livelihood there. His former slaves welcomed him back as the master, but bad health again plagued him, making plantation life impossible. The family then returned to Europe.

There seemed no end to his wanderings. In desperate financial straits, he returned to Memphis and accepted a position in the Mississippi Valley Association, a British company formed to induce European immigration into Mississippi by offering grants of land, and to finance a shipping line to ferry cotton across the Atlantic. Unable to raise the necessary capi-

The Davis children: Jefferson, Jr.,
Margaret, William, Winnie Anne

tal for these two enormous projects, the company was forced into liquidation.

Having reached the age of seventy in 1878, Davis was still enthusiastic and vigorous, enjoying better health than he had for years. His active career over, he retired to the Gulf Coast between New Orleans and Mobile. The State of Mississippi had just asked him to represent her in the Senate, but he was unable to accept since he was not a citizen.

From 1878 to 1881 Jefferson Davis worked on the history of the Confederacy, a two-volume book entitled *The Rise and Fall of the Confederate Government.* Commenting on this history, William E. Dodd wrote: "As a justification of secession

Varina Davis at Beauvoir

*Sketch of Oscar Wilde
by Varina Davis*

and the resulting Civil War, it is the best in existence; as an account of the military and civil events of the period, it is partisan and in some respects unreliable."

The Davises' pleasant home on the Gulf, "Beauvoir," became a gathering place. Among the many visitors was Oscar Wilde (of whom Varina made a sketch), Joseph Pulitzer, and Walter Hines Page. Meanwhile invitations to lecture had begun to pour in. In 1886 Davis spoke to enthusiastic audiences in various Southern states as well as in the West, and in so doing admitted that it was well the war had ended as it did. These trips were taken in style, special trains and guards of honor being provided; his progress through the South turned out to be "one prolonged ovation." The correspondent for the *New York World* wrote: "All the South is aflame, and where this triumphal march is to stop I cannot predict."

Varina Davis at 45

But these lecture tours exhausted Davis, and the fees were meager. A check for $250 from the *North American Review* for an article was a windfall. How pressed for funds he was is shown by his grateful acceptance of the gift of a twenty-dollar suit.

Davis was generous to a fault. Not only did he help support members of Varina's and his own family, but in his last years he even provided for the education of some poor children in the neighborhood of Beauvoir.

On June 3, 1888, Jefferson Davis quietly celebrated his eightieth birthday at Beauvoir. A correspondent from the *New Orleans Picayune* who was present reported that the one-time President of the Confederacy was "immaculately dressed, straight and erect, with traces of his military service still showing in his carriage and with the flush of health on his pale, refined face." The reporter added, "Jefferson Davis revealed a keen interest in current topics, political, social, religious."

The following year Davis came down with acute bronchitis and died in New Orleans on December 6, 1889. The funeral was the greatest the South had ever seen. Later his body was taken to Hollywood Cemetery in Richmond.

A great American had ended his career. He was a tragic figure, driven by his inflexible will to fight against impossible odds for a lost cause. He had to face problems far greater than Lincoln's. His faults were excessive intellectuality, an inclination to absolutes, and an insistence on deference. But if austere, he was also an extremely warm and gentle man. He had pluck and pertinacity, was thoughtful of others, and shrank from the sight of suffering. His wife Varina said of him, "Even a child's disappointment decomposed him."

In the stress of the Civil War, Jefferson Davis developed a New South, but he remained typical of that attractive way of living we think of as the Old South, and of an era of American chivalry that passed away. This finely wrought, sensitive man was—and remains—the symbol of a civilization that has disappeared as surely as the golden age of Louis XIV's France. Although the Southern economy was based on slavery, the Southern way of life was gracious and civilized.

The obituary of the President of the Confederacy that appeared in the *New York World* was short but eloquent: "A great soul has passed away." And the *London Herald* had observed as the Civil War ended: "Successful or fallen, tried or untried, condemned or uncondemned, Jefferson Davis is to us the greatest man in America."

Varina long survived her husband. She spent her last years in New York City, where she died in 1906.

Bibliography

The American Heritage Picture History of the Civil War. New York: American Heritage Publishing Co. Inc., 1960

BAEHR, HARRY W., JR. *The New York Tribune Since the Civil War.* New York: Dodd, Mead & Company, 1936

BOWERS, G. *The Tragic Era.* Cambridge: Houghton Mifflin Co., 1929

BRADFORD, GAMALIEL. *Confederate Portraits.* Boston: Houghton Mifflin Company, 1914

————. *Lee the American.* Boston: Houghton Mifflin Company, 1912

————. *Wives.* New York: Harper & Brothers, 1925

CATTON, BRUCE. *The Coming Fury.* New York: Doubleday & Co., 1961

————. *A Stillness at Appomattox.* New York: Doubleday & Company Inc., 1953.

CHESNUT, MARY BOYKIN. *A Diary from Dixie.* Boston: Houghton Mifflin Company, 1949

CRAVEN, BVT. LIEUT.-COL. DR. JOHN J. *Prison Life of Jefferson Davis.* New York: Carleton Publisher, 1866

CUTTING, ELISABETH. *Jefferson Davis Political Soldier.* New York: Dodd, Mead and Company, 1930

DAVIS, JEFFERSON. *The Rise and Fall of the Confederate Government.* New York: D. Appleton and Co., 1881

DAVIS, VARINA. *Jefferson Davis, ex-President of the Confederate States of America; a memoir by his wife.* 2 vols. New York: Belfort Company, 1890

The Diary of Philip Hone (1828–1851). Edited, with an introduction by Allan Nevins. New York: Dodd, Mead and Company, 1927

DODD, WILLIAM E. *Jefferson Davis.* Philadelphia: George W. Jacobs & Company, 1907

EATON, CLEMENT. *Jefferson Davis.* New York: Macmillan Publishing Co., 1977

ECKENRODE, H. J. *Jefferson Davis President of the South.* New York: The Macmillan Company, 1923

FREEMAN, DOUGLAS SOUTHALL and MC SHINEY, GRADY, Editors. *Lee's Dispatches, 1862–5.* New York: G. P. Putnam's Sons, 1957

GARRATY, JOHN A. *The American Nation: A History of the United States.* New York: Harper & Row and American Heritage Publishing Co., 1966

GREELEY, HORACE. *The American Conflict.* Vol. I. Chicago: O. D. Case & Company, 1864

GUTMAN, HERBERT G. *The Black Family in Slavery and Freedom, 1750–1925.* New York: Pantheon Books, 1976

HELPER, HINTON R. *The Impending Crisis of the South.* New York: A. B. Burdick, 1860

JONES, KATHARINE M. *Ladies of Richmond.* New York: Bobbs-Merrill Company, Inc., 1962

KIMMEL, STANLEY. *Mr. Davis's Richmond.* New York: Coward McCann, 1958

LAWRENCE, VERA BRODSKY. *Music for Patriots, Politicians, and Presidents.* New York: Macmillan Publishing Co., Inc., 1975

LECKIE, ROBERT. *The Wars of America.* New York: Harper & Row, 1968

MC ELROY, ROBERT. *Jefferson Davis, the Unreal and the Real.* New York: Harper & Brothers Publishers, 1937

MORISON, SAMUEL ELIOT. *The Oxford History of the United States.* New York: Oxford University Press, 1965

ROSS, ISHBEL. *First Lady of the South.* New York: Harper & Brothers, 1958

———. *Rebel Rose.* New York: Harper & Brothers, 1954

SCHAFF, MORRIS. *Jefferson Davis—His Life and Personality.* Boston: John W. Luce & Co., 1922

STAMPP, KENNETH M. *The Peculiar Institution.* New York: Alfred Knopf, 1956

STEPHENS, ALEXANDER H. *A Constitutional View of the Late War Between the States.* Vol. I. Philadelphia: National Publishing Company, 1868

STRODE, HUDSON. *Jefferson Davis: American Patriot 1808–61.* New York: Harcourt Brace & Company, 1955

———. *Jefferson Davis: Confederate President.* New York: Harcourt Brace & Company, 1959

———. *Jefferson Davis: Private Letters 1823–1889.* New York: Harcourt Brace & World, 1966

———. *Jefferson Davis: Tragic Hero 1864–89.* New York: Harcourt Brace & Company, 1964

TATE, ALLEN. *Jefferson Davis—His Rise and Fall.* New York: Minton, Balch & Company, 1964

THOMAS, EMORY. *The Confederacy.* New York: Harper & Row, 1977

TROWBRIDGE, JOHN T. *The Desolate South 1865–1866.* Edited by Gordon Carroll. New York: Duell, Sloan and Pearce, Inc. 1956

WEEKS, STEPHEN B. *Southern Quakers and Slavery.* Baltimore: The Johns Hopkins Press, 1896

WERSTEIN, IRVING. *Abraham Lincoln Versus Jefferson Davis.* New York: T. Y. Crowell Co., 1959

WHITTON, MARY ORMSBEE. *These Were the Women. U.S.A. 1776–1860.* New York: Hastings House Publishers, 1954

WILEY, BELL, and HIRST MILHOLLEN. *Embattled Confederates.* New York: Harper & Row, 1964

WINSTON, ROBERT W. *High Stakes and Hair Trigger.* New York: Henry Holt and Company, 1930

Index